Breaking the POVERTY BARRIER

CHANGING STUDENT LIVES WITH
PASSION, PERSEVERANCE,
AND PERFORMANCE

RICARDO LEBLANC-ESPARZA & WILLIAM S. ROULSTON

Solution Tree | Press

a division of

Solution Tree

555 North Morton Street
Bloomington, IN 47404
800.733.6786 (toll free) / 812.336.7700
FAX: 812.336.7790

email: info@solution-tree.com
solution-tree.com

Visit **go.solution-tree.com/schoolimprovement** to download the reproducibles in this book.

Printed in the United States of America

15 14 13 12 11   1 2 3 4 5

Library of Congress Cataloging-in-Publication Data

LeBlanc-Esparza, Ricardo.

  Breaking the poverty barrier : changing student lives with passion, perseverance, and performance / Ricardo LeBlanc-Esparza, William S. Roulston.

     p. cm.

  Includes bibliographical references.

  ISBN 978-1-935543-14-5 (perfect bound) -- ISBN 978-1-935543-15-2 (library edition)
1. LeBlanc-Esparza, Ricardo. 2. School principals--Washington (State)--Granger.
3. Granger High School (Granger, WA) 4. Educational change--Washington (State)-
-Granger. 5. School Improvement Programs--Washington (State)--Granger. 6. Poor
children--Education--Washington (State)--Granger. 7. Children with social disabilities-
-Education--Washington (State)--Granger. 8. Educational change--United States. I.
Roulston, William S. II. Title.
  LA2317.L44A3 2012
  371.2'07--dc23
                                    2011020056

Solution Tree
Jeffrey C. Jones, CEO & President

Solution Tree Press
President: Douglas M. Rife
Publisher: Robert D. Clouse
Vice President of Production: Gretchen Knapp
Managing Production Editor: Caroline Wise
Senior Production Editor: Lesley Bolton
Text Designer: Amy Shock
Cover Designer: Jenn Taylor

Ricardo LeBlanc-Esparza

To my beautiful wife, to whom I owe fifty-two more years on a contract that I will do my best to uphold: thank you for believing in me and my mission of trying to change our country into a better place for all people.

William S. Roulston

To the children striving to know and live more fully: this is all for you.

To the strong teachers—independent, creative, and loving—who labor to help them: nothing happens without you.

To the wise principals who support their teachers and, in turn, need our support: everything depends on you.

ACKNOWLEDGMENTS

Ricardo LeBlanc-Esparza

I would like to recognize the following people, who have made a difference in my life and have been part of my journey of trying to make a difference for students, parents, educators, and community. I would like to thank:

My fifth-grade teacher, Mrs. Martin, who told me that I had good writing skills and should continue to write; my middle school science teacher, Mr. Schwabauer, who told me I had good speaking skills and encouraged me to look into a career that involved public speaking; my wrestling coach, Rich Leenhouts, who encouraged me to go to college because I had "potential"; and finally, my college wrestling coach, Eric Beardsley, who taught me to believe in myself and to work hard to accomplish goals

My friends who never stopped believing in me and my crazy dream of publishing a book that would make a difference for public education

My family and kids, Richard Esparza, Natasha Esparza, Sara LeBlanc, and Kayleigh LeBlanc, for putting up with me through this long process of trying to find my path

The students, staff, and community of Granger High School for their willingness to fight for a dream that all students can reach their potential in a positive learning environment

Kati Haycock at Education Trust for her support of our work, and Karin Chenoweth for her support and advice

My coauthor, William Roulston, for standing by me through the good, bad, and ugly of fighting through turning around a school and writing this book

And finally, my parents, Cipriano and Dominga Esparza, for their love, guidance, and never-ending support, which helped me become who I am today

William S. Roulston

Thanks to my first principal at Nob Hill Elementary, the late Harvey Stevenson, who was the perfect example of a one-life-at-a-time principal and surely helped this young boy grow. Jane Schwab, you made the most indelible mark of any of my teachers by seeing something special inside me and asking this jock to consider becoming your TA so I could help other young men discover the beauty of the written word. Jim Connor, a true man, you helped me think about the possibilities of being a teacher. Lee White, although I didn't prove to be a great chemistry student, you gave selflessly to me on the track; you used sports and your belief in me to teach me lessons that I find myself going back to even now so that I can recenter when life gets off-kilter. Elinor Michel, thanks for shaping me as a writer.

Dave Smith of Mullan Jr/Sr High School, Jerry Craig of West Valley High School, and Gary Fendell of White Swan High School: exemplary principals all.

Sandra Pasiero Davis, you gave me the chance to grow as a consultant and knew just the right way to manage my mercurial spirit. Marsha Ann Pastrana and Sid Turner, you were the most delightful collaborators I have ever worked with, and Elma Rodriguez, Sandy Nyberg, and Carol Hawthorne, thank you for your support. To my regional collaborators—Ismael Vivanco, Tatiana Gabriel, Sylvia Reyna, and Mike Taylor—I am eternally grateful for who you are. Barbara Lawson and Phyllis Keilly-Tyler: thanks.

Special thanks to the late Ruth Cole for introducing me to Second Shot Reading and to Chris Mayfield, Lora Anderson, and Jan Bolson, the paraeducators who helped keep it alive after Ruth's untimely passing.

Thanks to Claudia Wheatley for first introducing Ricardo to Solution Tree, to Douglas Rife for believing in our story, and to Lesley Bolton for her incredible skill in bringing clarity to our manuscript and helping our writing to flow.

Thanks the best principal I ever worked with, my coauthor, Ricardo. You continue to teach and inspire me. I'm proud to be your partner in the battle. Viva la revolución!

Most of all, thanks to my family. Tania Maria and Nico: look! Dreams can come true when you stick with them. Dr. George Roulston: you're the best act a guy could follow. Delila Roulston: more than anyone, you gave me the gift of language.

Solution Tree Press would like to thank the following reviewers:

Trudy Grafton
Principal
Study Elementary School
Fort Wayne, Indiana

Lou Howell
Executive Director
Iowa Association for Curriculum and Staff Development
Des Moines, Iowa

Visit **go.solution-tree.com/schoolimprovement** to download the reproducibles in this book.

TABLE OF CONTENTS

ABOUT THE AUTHORS

 **Ricardo LeBlanc-Esparza** is a school change coach at the Center for Secondary School Redesign in West Warwick, Rhode Island. With twenty-nine years of experience in high-poverty schools, Ricardo has been an alternative high school principal, high school principal, assistant principal, athletic director, teacher, and coach. When Ricardo began serving as principal of Granger High in the state of Washington, the school had a 30 percent graduation rate and the community had the highest reported crime rate in the region. By developing a team approach that involved parents, students, educators, and the community working toward a common goal, he helped Granger High achieve a 90 percent graduation rate, and the crime rate in the community decreased.

Ricardo was named 2007, 2005, and 2002 Principal of the Year, 1996 Athletic Director of the Year, and 1990 Coach of the Year. He has given dozens of presentations and has written for numerous educational publications.

Ricardo earned bachelor's and master's degrees from Central Washington University.

 **Will Roulston** taught English, Spanish, reading, resource room, drama, and English as a second language (ESL) at high schools and middle schools in Washington and Idaho and developed his background in school turnaround at the Migrant Education Office at Educational Service District 105 in Yakima, Washington. Working to support thirty school districts, he synthesized research and collaborated with administrators, teachers, and others to improve the learning of impoverished and minority students as well as English learners. His projects included elementary and secondary literacy, assessment, English language acquisition, and school leadership. He also presented regionally and nationally at conferences, coached and modeled effective instruction in

local classrooms, and created the Second Shot Reading Foundation, dedicated to helping teenaged struggling readers.

Will first did consulting work at Granger High School in 1999. Two years later, he went to work there full time as a reading teacher and staff-development coach, working alongside Ricardo until 2004. From 2004 to 2009, he took a sabbatical to make a documentary film, *DreamRiders*, winning awards at film festivals and appearing on television. He has returned to helping schools through his writing, presenting, and consulting.

To book Ricardo LeBlanc-Esparza or William S. Roulston for professional development, contact pd@solution-tree.com.

PREFACE

I hope this book will change your professional life as much as mine was changed on the day I met my coauthor, Ricardo LeBlanc-Esparza.

I was on my way back from doing some consultation work with a school about ninety miles from home when my office called and told me to stop by Grandview High School. An assistant principal, a Mr. Esparza, needed help with raising his students' reading scores, and he had heard that I was the man he needed to talk to. An hour later, I walked into his office and knew immediately that I liked him and that the feeling was mutual. What I didn't know was that an astounding adventure lay ahead of us.

Over the next year, as we worked on ways to turn around his high school, we came to realize that we shared many of the same beliefs about how to help students be more successful and what changes needed to take place in schools to actually accomplish that feat. As iron sharpens iron, we sharpened and clarified our thinking as we bounced ideas off each other, articulating more clearly what we saw as the critical difference makers. I brought with me the vantage point of working with thirty school districts in our region that were all trying to raise student achievement, and Ricardo had the perspective of a frontline general.

When he called me the next summer and told me he had been offered a new job as principal of Granger High School, my advice was simple: don't take it. I was very well acquainted with the Granger School District. It was the one district out of thirty that I no longer delivered services to. I liked the people there, who seemed to love my workshops and kept inviting me back, but I had never seen a place with poorer follow-through. Each time I went back, I noticed that nothing had changed. It seemed like the whole district was so discouraged by the lack of student success that they were just going through the motions. Even though some people have called me a hyperoptimist, something was so badly fouled up with their system that I gave up hope of it ever changing. I thought Granger High School would eat my partner alive.

Thankfully, Ricardo, stubborn all-American wrestler that he is, did not take my advice. Soon after he took the job, he had me going back to the high school to help him set his plans in motion. For two years, I was a frequent presence, leading professional development in literacy and language acquisition strategies with his teachers. Finally, one of the teachers said something to me that I'm sure many teachers would love to say to workshop presenters: "If you really think these strategies will work with our kids, then you should come here and teach. Show me you can do it with our kids. Then I'll believe it." So I did. For the next three years, I taught reading and drama and continued to lead professional development. Ricardo kept placing me on committees for school improvement and other district initiatives so we could continue working together to make systemic changes. Most importantly, I was now on the front lines, working directly with the students and parents who needed education and with the teachers whose job it was to provide it.

In June 2004, I left Granger High for an opportunity to make a documentary film with my son on a social issue of great importance to me. Over the next four years, I watched from afar as Ricardo continued the journey, confronting and overcoming problems one at a time, relentlessly marching toward his mission of preparing 100 percent of his students for success in postsecondary education. The results were remarkable. I personally have heard of no greater turnaround of a school in similarly dire circumstances, and I've done a fair amount of searching.

When he left Granger in June 2008, Ricardo called on me once again, this time to write this book. Once again, we went through the process we had experienced early in our partnership. Through the power of reflective conversation and with the benefit of hindsight, we were able to articulate more clearly what we saw as the critical differences between what we had done at Granger High School and the improvement efforts we had seen at so many other schools. Looking back at the journey, we knew that we had to go through all our painful trials in order to learn what we learned, but we wished we had known then what we know now. Our process would have been much faster and easier; we would have started the journey with the confidence that our ideas had been tested and proven; and we would have known how to explain better to our colleagues what we were trying to do.

Now it's time for your school. Our sole purpose in writing this book was to help more people do exactly what we did. We want to immerse readers in our experiences and name for them the critical things we learned, the subtle nuances between successful and less successful practices, and the beliefs and ways of thinking that guided our actions. The end result of nine years of experience at Granger High School and nearly two years of effort in writing this book is this: I have an absolute belief that other schools can do this, too.

Do principles transcend principals? I believe that we couldn't have turned around our school without a truly unique individual like Ricardo. Turnaround leadership is vital for turnaround schools. However, I also believe it was the power of our ideas that made the difference. Force of will, something Ricardo has in abundance, is only helpful when it's forcing people toward right actions, and right actions are born from the inevitable logic of right thinking. Whether you're a district leader, a school leader, a classroom leader, or a community leader, I hope that our principles will allow you to transcend whatever obstacles stand between your students and success.

William S. Roulston

April 2011

INTRODUCTION

A *New York Times* article dated August 10, 2010, stated that the U.S. government "has sharply increased federal financing for school turnarounds, to $3.5 billion this year, about 28 times as much as in 2007. Secretary of Education Arne Duncan is pushing to overhaul 5,000 of the nation's 100,000 public schools in the next few years." But the article highlights a problem: "Companies with little or no experience are portraying themselves as school-turnaround experts as they compete for the money" (Dillon, 2010).

That's understandable. The demand for help is great, and few service providers have seen their ideas turned into reality in actual school buildings. Most providers haven't had their hands directly on the controls of a failing school, and most haven't shown by their test data that they know how to turn it around.

Will Roulston and I were fortunate enough to have participated in a school turnaround process that changed the lives of students who otherwise would have likely been sentenced to a life of poverty. Granger High School was a public, open-enrollment high school in which 90 percent of the students participated in the free and reduced lunch program and in which 90 percent of the students were students of color. Because of the turnaround, many students became the first high school graduates in their families, and a large number of graduates went on to postsecondary education and good careers. With diplomas in hand, these former students are now breaking the cycle of poverty that they were born into.

And that is the prime motivation that drove us to write. We want to help all students succeed, even the most impoverished students who challenge our educational systems so greatly. Here are some of the ways in which we helped turn around exactly those kinds of students:

- We developed strong leadership that got people working together.
- We involved parents in managing their children's education.
- We mentored students to make sure they knew why they were studying.
- We used data to determine what we needed to do better and implemented strategic literacy interventions, schoolwide instructional

strategies suited for our population, and professional learning communities for staff.

- We transformed negative belief systems and created a culture of success.

If you find yourself leading or teaching in a school that needs improved achievement results and increased graduation rates, welcome aboard. We hope you find this book different from most books on the subject of school turnarounds. We love the inspirational stories about educators' journeys, but those stories leave us woefully short of understanding the specific strategies that made the journey possible. And unfortunately, the how-to books don't provide the critical, gritty stories that reveal the insights and aha moments, the fine distinctions that get to the heart of the matter and show how seemingly similar strategies are really quite different in effectiveness. That's why this book is a hybrid of a journey story and a how-to book.

In chapter 1, we explain why our school was considered a failing school. We detail how low we started and then show you how high we climbed in the process of our turnaround. Chapter 2 describes the serious business of leadership: the kind needed for the job of turning around a low-performing school and how it can be developed through adopting the critical core beliefs that lie at the heart of effective leadership. Chapter 3 details how to get students and their parents to join your staff in an unstoppable team that supports student achievement, explaining the simple, replicable strategies we used to make progress toward success. Chapter 4 describes why our school needed a mentorship program and explains how it worked.

Chapter 5 contains a detailed explanation of our primary reading intervention, Rewire Reading. Readers interested in building a similar customized approach will find this chapter to be a wealth of information because it both unlocks the strategies used and links them to theoretical models of why readers struggle, particularly older students. Chapter 6 is a collection of other interventions we implemented—our revamped English curriculum, the other two prongs of our three-pronged literacy program, the use of one specific strategy across the curriculum to improve learning for all our students, and extended learning time and built-in mechanisms to make sure students were working hard, both in class and out.

Chapter 7 focuses on an oft-neglected side of turning around any school or organization: creating change from the inside out. This chapter details the importance of changing the negative beliefs, attitudes, and traditions in a failing school and then shows the steps taken to actually accomplish it. Chapter 8 explores how our turnaround strategy is applicable to schools that are different from ours and presents a series of guiding questions to use in planning your own turnaround. The appendix includes a few reproducible letters we mention throughout the book. Visit **go.solution-tree.com/schoolimprovement** to download the reproducibles and for an outline of the book that will assist you in creating plans for your own turnaround efforts.

Chapter 1

FROM NOT-SO-GOOD TO GREAT

"This is the noisiest, angriest school I have ever been in." That was the recurring thought going through my mind during my first week as the new principal of Granger High School. Teachers yelled at students, and often students yelled back; students yelled at students; teachers even yelled at each other. It would not be long before they were yelling at me.

I'd been warned about coming to this small high school of 330 students in the Yakima Valley, an agricultural region of Washington.

I had heard people refer to Granger as the "armpit of the Valley," usually pointing out some of the high-profile murders that had occurred there. One of those murders had actually taken place on the high school campus; a student was knifed in the student parking lot and died in the gymnasium. Granger was a tagged town, the gang graffiti that proliferated on any flat surface providing a good clue to what was happening. Several of the teachers joked that if Granger High School wasn't lowest in the state in test scores, then a neighboring school was. Apparently, it was a tight race each year, and nobody seemed to be working too hard to pull ahead.

Consider the following statistics from my first year, 1999:

- The percentage of incoming freshmen who met state standards (when they were last tested in seventh grade) was 2 percent in reading, 2 percent in writing, and 1 percent in math.

- Our graduation rate was somewhere below 50 percent. (Our documented graduation rate was 58 percent. However, that figure was based on comparing the number of seniors at the beginning of the year to how many actually graduated. It did not count all the students who dropped out in their freshman, sophomore, or junior years. We estimated that the real rate was well below 50 percent. The 90 percent graduation rate we increased to was based on a true reflection of percent of entering freshmen who ended up graduating.)

- Approximately 90 percent of our students were students of color, mostly Latino and some Native American students.

- About 90 percent of our students qualified for free or reduced lunch.

- About 70 percent of parents of students hadn't graduated from high school.

- Roughly 10 percent of parents attended parent conferences to talk about their children's futures.

- Law enforcement statistics showed that the Granger community had the highest reported crime rate per capita of any town in the area (Courtney, 2004).

By 2008, the picture had changed dramatically. Table 1.1 shows the outcome of everyone's hard work.

Table 1.1: Before-and-After Comparison of Our Turnaround School

Before	After
Incoming freshmen who met state standards: 2% reading, 2% writing, and 1% math	Sophomores meeting standards rose to 77% reading, 67% writing, and 31% math, even though middle school scores never rose above 10–20% in reading and writing or above 5% in math
Graduation rate below 50%	Average graduation rate of 90%
90% students of color	No change
90% students of poverty	No change
70% of parents were not high school grads	70% of students applied for postsecondary education
10% parent attendance at conferences	100% parent attendance at conferences
Community had highest crime rate in the area (Courtney, 2004)	Crime rate dropped to lowest in the area

The Office of Superintendent of Public Instruction for the State of Washington (OSPI) named us a National Model High School in 2004 and 2006. The Center for Secondary School Redesign awarded us the title of National Showcase High School in 2007 and 2008. And the Education Trust, an organization that provides research and advocates for closing the achievement gap, invited Will and me to present in Washington, DC, to explain how we were able to make such gains. We came across some interesting information as we prepared our presentation.

In his book *Class and Schools: Using Social, Economic, and Educational Reform to Close the Black-White Achievement Gap*, Richard Rothstein (2004), a researcher at the Economic Policy Institute and a lecturer at Columbia University's Teachers

College, builds a convincing case for the effect of social class, which involves factors of race, income, and social and cultural status, on education. I agree that students from lower social classes are more likely to suffer from poor health, mobility, unstable/substandard housing, lack of educated caretakers and role models, and even lowered early IQs—all of which are difficult obstacles to overcome. But then Rothstein says, "The influence of social class characteristics is probably so powerful that schools cannot overcome it, no matter how well trained are their teachers and no matter how well designed are their instructional programs and climates" (p. 5).

It gave us great pleasure at our presentation to respectfully disagree with that statement and back it up with our data. We went on to share some important observations about our success, as well as some hard-earned wisdom that anyone wishing to follow in our school-turnaround footsteps needs to know.

It's not the strategy you use; it's how you use it that makes the difference. For example, we succeeded in getting 100 percent of our students' parents to attend parent conferences. Our feeder middle school took our ideas for parent involvement and claimed that they got 90 percent of their parents to attend conferences. Great news! But why didn't they get the same results that we got in our classrooms? Why did their test scores barely change? What happened? They ran their conferences in a group setting and not as individual conferences; they did not make individual connections. In our view, they missed the point when it came to parent conferences: building personal, collaborative relationships that ensure responsibility. That is one of the core beliefs that drove our parent conferences, and when that core belief was not honored, our middle school's efforts were unsuccessful.

The answer is not in buying the right program. When government, corporations, and foundations target special needs with special funding, in our experience, most schools use it to buy a program. What happens, however, is that we buy the program with hopes of making beautiful music like Stravinsky's *Symphony of Psalms*, but we take only enough lessons to get "Three Blind Mice." Practitioners don't develop true expertise with the program, so they don't get the desired result. With the billions of dollars currently available to turn around our schools, the temptation will be even greater to buy our way out of failure, but we don't think it's possible to do it that way. As famed basketball coach John Wooden liked to tell his players, "Never mistake activity for achievement."

School turnarounds often fail because they use a bits-and-pieces approach. So much good advice is out there, in books and from consultants, about how to improve schools. I'm sure this is not the first book you've read this year on improving your school. However, the effect of taking in all this good (and sometimes conflicting) advice is often the lack of a cohesive approach to reform. We get so busy saving individual trees that we don't notice that the whole forest is on fire.

Certainly, this book offers specific strategies, but we want you to see the forest we cultivated to contain them. For example, we used a literacy intervention, which by itself was powerful in turning around students' lack of reading skills and increasing their confidence as learners—but it was only one-third of the power of our literacy program. If another school were to implement that intervention without the other two-thirds of the literacy program, they simply could not achieve our results. Beyond that, we would not have achieved the same amount of success if we focused on our three-pronged literacy program only. We needed the impact of parent communication systems, mentorships, mechanisms in our system to ensure high engagement and accountability, cross-curricular learning tools, and the other ideas this book details in order to maximize the benefits gained from implementing literacy improvements. When it came to our school turnaround, the whole really was greater than the sum of the parts.   ← important

We're confident that any school that truly wants to revolutionize its students' learning can study our specific strategies with an eye to understanding why they worked, plan how to implement the key elements in a way that makes sense for their school culture and history, and then, with a few years of disciplined effort, realize equal or better results.

For those who feel lost or at a loss when confronting the daunting terrain ahead, our road map gives you the tools to navigate it successfully. Your school's current best doesn't have to be its future best.

Chapter 2

LEADING THE TURNAROUND

One of my professors asked me to do a presentation for one of his master's classes. During the question-and-answer session, one of his students asked, "Do you think you could do it again? I mean, if you went to a new school that was struggling just as much and started all over, could you get the same results?" She then reminded me that even Jaime Escalante, whose story was featured in the movie *Stand and Deliver* (Musca & Menéndez, 1988), was unable to duplicate his success when he moved to a new school. The challenges facing us are daunting. Students are so discouraged that they drop out at the rate of 1.2 million every year (Editorial Projects in Education, 2007).

"Could we do it again?" I repeated to my questioner. "Yes. We absolutely could do it again."

My conviction since that day has only grown stronger as I've studied what the experts say about leadership and school transformation. I now see even more clearly why what we did in the face of so much adversity worked as well as it did.

The more important question, however, is the one that the student left unasked that day. I suspect that when she asked if I could lead a repeat performance, she had another question in mind, something a little more personal: "Do you think *I* could do what you did in your school?"

If you're asking the same thing, my answer is yes.

Absolutely, yes, because what we did was not magic, and neither was what Escalante accomplished at Garfield High School in East Los Angeles. Oh, I know that a two-hour movie with gifted actors can make the transformation seem like magic, but having been behind the scenes of our own school-improvement drama, I know it's not.

Escalante really did what he did; that was no illusion. He built an amazing legacy of success with an AP calculus program in a high-poverty school. And we really did what we did; we turned around, not just a classroom, but a whole school beset by poverty and failure. In the book *Escalante: The Best Teacher in America*, Jay Matthews (1989) reveals the secrets that the movie mutes or even obscures. The secrets that made Escalante successful, as I see them, are what made us successful, too, and they are the same secrets that I see when I read school-improvement literature. The secrets are:

- Have a strong set of core beliefs, and spread them and live them daily.
- Have strong leadership.
- Use systems approaches.

The rest of this book elaborates on these elements, with this chapter focusing on the core beliefs that drove us and the leadership strategies we used. These three secrets may not seem like secrets to you, but allow us to explore them and show them to you through our eyes. Most educators we know, ourselves included, just want the facts. We already know our craft pretty well, and we're pretty darn busy. We take on a kind of checklist mentality to stay on schedule: "Yes, I know that. Yup, we do that already. Okay, there's one I should probably try. Next." We would submit that subtle differences exist between what we did and your experiences. They are differences of a degree or nuance that deserve deeper inspection. To that end, we share stories and give examples to help you understand with both your head and your heart what we think really makes the difference. Head and heart: the key to replicating our success comes from understanding the thoughts and actions that emanate from both.

This chapter is written from a principal's point of view, but much of the information applies directly to other administrators and classroom leaders. We encourage teachers to translate the examples in ways that will help them create and sustain change with their students because teachers, of course, are the most important leaders of all.

Leadership and Core Beliefs

Can good leadership be replicated? Some people claim that we need to clone good leaders, and others say it is impossible, either literally or metaphorically, to clone leadership. To be sure, leadership is a complex, multifaceted creature that mixes personality, communication and conflict resolution skills, the ability to relate to others, character, integrity, drive, and so on. There are many variables, but there are also some constants: the core beliefs that I believe provide the best possible chance of replicating successful leadership.

I believe we all operate on basic core beliefs that we have developed throughout our lives, and we base our decisions on these beliefs, even when we're not fully aware of what they are. These "mental models" (Preskill & Torres, 1999) created through our experiences frame our perspectives. Two things have primarily influenced my mental models: poverty and sports.

Today, I feel fortunate that I grew up in poverty because of how it prepared me to work with impoverished schools. My family was poor until around the time

I entered middle school, although I didn't know it at first because I ate three meals a day and always had a roof over my head. Sure, we moved from place to place and lived with relatives a lot so that my parents could work, but that seemed normal. I thought everyone slept three to a bed with their cousins or camped out together on the floor. Now I understand that we were migrants out of economic necessity.

I was in elementary school when I noticed for the first time that our family did not have as much as other families. My first indication was the realization that my box of crayons contained only eight crayons. The kids around me all seemed to have the elite box of sixty-four crayons with the built-in sharpener. At recess, it dawned on me that many of the other kids had no patches on their pants. I don't think these differences bothered me much because all of my relatives were in the same situation. My social life consisted of visiting relatives, having family barbecues, and working in the fields, and no one ever talked about whether you had a crayon sharpener or not.

My family was able to work their way out of a life of poverty by the time I reached seventh grade, a milestone I remember clearly because some of my friends told me that I was now one of those "rich" kids. The criterion for their judgment was that I no longer wore patches on my pants. In reality, we had moved from poverty to lower middle class, but to other poor people, it seemed like a huge jump.

Just as I did not realize when I was younger that I was poor, I did not fully realize while I was at Granger that my upbringing had caused me to develop ways of looking at the world that were different from the views of many educators, and those differences were so critical in reaching students who had little money and few resources.

My experiences as a competitive wrestler also shaped my beliefs. Drive, determination, and a razor-sharp awareness of the slightest weakness in an opponent were the keys to performing successfully in the heat of the battle. My learning continued later in my stints as a coach and a high school athletic director. I found that sometimes, as much as they didn't like it at first, I needed to push people because they wanted to go their own way instead of the way of the team or to avoid the work they needed to do to achieve their potential. Those experiences were like a real-world laboratory for me. Through trial and error, action, and observation, I formed beliefs about how to work with people to get results and motivate them to improve their lives, especially individuals who were like I once was: on the bottom, looking up.

Most educators have never been on the bottom, looking up, in school. And unless they've experienced significant success with their hard-to-reach students, it's not only likely but also logical that doubts have crept in: can students on the bottom really be successful? More important but harder to ask is: can *I* be successful with them? If you have doubts, if little "yeah buts" and excuses that rationalize your past results pop into your mind as you read, then take the time to examine the beliefs and leadership strategies in this chapter with a razor-sharp awareness of the small differences between these beliefs and yours.

Core Belief 1

You must find your driving passion and let it color everything you do.

I knew what my mission was, and I felt so passionately about accomplishing it that I could not give up, even when I wanted to. Over the years, as I thought about my students and the problems they faced, I inevitably went back to my own past. I thought most frequently about my grandparents. They were good, loving, honest, and hardworking people who babysat me when I was too young to go to the fields with my parents, and I loved them dearly. I didn't realize they were poor until my own family rose into the working class. Then it was clear that not only were they born in poverty, but also that they continued to live the rest of their lives in poverty. To come home from college and see these wonderful people be rewarded for all their toil with Social Security checks that barely enabled them to survive after they were too old and feeble to work, well, that hurt. They never had the opportunity to get an education, to develop skills that an employer would find attractive enough to pay them a higher wage. They worked hard; they loved their children hard; and they died hard.

My passion is to never let a student of mine be doomed to a life of poverty. I know that education is a child's best hope. If we don't give students advanced learning skills while they're with us, they most likely will never develop them and will be stuck in poverty. I can picture them looking at me years from now through old and sad eyes, asking me, "Why didn't you tell me how it was going to be? You could have helped me."

That's the image that kept me fighting when I got tired. Those are the voices that told me to focus on the right priorities when making decisions. Granger High School was not just a job to me; it was a cause, a quest, a chance to break the poverty cycle for a whole generation of students in my care. This is my passion.

What is your passion? Do you have a crystal-clear mission that makes showing up at work each day about more than just getting a paycheck? What is that something that excites you and actually makes your job—dare I say it—fun? If you have a driving passion, it will guide your every decision, helping you to stand strong when you face challenges, and it will seep into every conversation with staff, students, and parents. If you don't have a passion, discover it. Create it. It's never too late.

Core Belief 2

All students are capable of learning at their highest potential when expected to do so in a positive learning environment.

This core belief doesn't sound controversial until you read the thoughts of people such as David Berliner (2009) from Arizona State University. In his paper *Poverty and Potential: Out-of-School Factors and School Success*, he says, "Poverty limits student potential; inputs to schools affect outputs from them" (p. 1).

Look at the first half of that sentence. It sounds like an ironclad rule that if you grow up in poverty, you have limited potential in comparison to those who grow up in the middle class or higher. Researchers such as Berliner and Richard Rothstein (2004) have a lot of data showing that students of poverty don't achieve as high on average as higher socioeconomic status (SES) students. We don't dispute that.

But why aim to build an average program that produces average results? We aimed to build a superior program, and it far exceeded the average of what impoverished and minority students accomplished elsewhere. Why handicap your mission at the very outset by believing that your students are limited?

If you look at this core belief carefully, you'll notice that the most important thing isn't the caliber of student that comes to us—the "input," to borrow Berliner's term. We can't control the input, but we can control our expectations and the kind of learning environment (system) that we create for students.

The phrase *all students are capable of learning* speaks of potential. The idea that all students are *expected* to learn demands that potential is realized and turns a dreamy ideal into a cold, hard reality. We changed our mission statement from "All students will be given the opportunity to reach their academic and social potential in a positive learning environment" to "All students will be expected to reach …" This small shift in emphasis got to the real point and made sure we didn't let ourselves off the hook.

More importantly, this change in emphasis didn't let our students and parents off the hook either. In an era in which schools are in danger of being taken over or dismantled if they don't meet standards, principals are fired, and teachers are increasingly evaluated on their students' performance, we need to hold students and their parents accountable, too. The three-way communication system that we will describe in chapter 3 was our primary method of bringing this accountability into reality, but it started with the core belief that all students are *expected* to learn. With the backing of our mission statement, we could tell students (and their parents), "Look, this is our mission. Are you learning to your potential? Are we wrong to expect you to do so?"

But believing that all students can learn and expecting them to do so are not enough by themselves. It's our responsibility to create the positive learning environment that supports their achievement. That environment must provide everything they need in order to learn, and it must eliminate excuses. The more systematic we can make it, the better. As we discuss throughout the book, the systems we put in place need mechanisms that operate as fail-safes. Without such mechanisms, the educational system is too big, and students will get lost or forgotten despite our best intentions and planning. After putting these mechanisms in place, we must be ever vigilant of the roadblocks for individual students and adjust the educational environment for them. (We explain the systems and the mechanisms we created in the chapters that follow.)

Core Belief 3

You must craft your mission and goals carefully, then sell, sell, sell!

Mark Twain once said, "The difference between the almost right word and the right word is really a large matter—it's the difference between the lightning bug and the lightning." The same is true of how we express our mission; it can be either an awesomely powerful force, shaking sky and earth, or a harmless little glow in the backyard on a summer's eve. Changing the phrase "all students will be given the opportunity" to learn in the mission statement to "all students will be expected" to learn was an important step. But to be powerful, this statement also needed to be attainable.

Therefore, we created a goal: "to help 100 percent of our students have the necessary skills to move on to postsecondary education." We kept our *mission* statement as written because it expressed important truths that we needed to be reminded of at times, but our *goal* statement was the down-and-dirty, show-up-for-work-every-day kind of idea that we needed to do the job.

After we had a clear and simple goal statement, we had to sell it. Just like the thick curriculum realignment notebooks that district committees put together and then sit unopened on the shelves of every teacher, our goal would have no effect if it stayed hidden in the minutes from our staff meetings. Our goal was clear, and we communicated it consistently to parents, students, educators, and community members. I reiterated this goal in memos to staff. We made posters of our goal and hung them all over the school. I wrote about it in newsletters. We reminded students of it in assemblies.

This goal permeated my conversations. Whenever I was questioned about a decision I made, I always went back to our goal and reminded my questioner of what we were striving for in common. I cannot tell you the number of times this reminder of commonality defused disagreements and kept us from fighting through unnecessary battles. And in cases in which the battle was necessary, the goal helped me to stand firm when there was no room for compromise.

To achieve your ultimate objective, you must create a clear, simple, and attainable goal statement and use it like a mantra, repeating it over and over until you reach that goal. The more in agreement that each member of your team is with your goal—and by *team*, I mean staff, parents, and students—the more the goal will be on their hearts and the easier it will be to accomplish the mission. This agreement is a critical part of getting people to fly in perfect formation, using the efficiency that many bodies moving in the same direction creates, cutting the wind resistance that individuals must battle when having to fly their own separate ways to reach the same destination.

Core Belief 4

Teachers must be supported and held to high expectations for their students' learning.

As with core belief 2, this principle is not just a nice platitude. We must give this belief muscle in the real world by doing the same two things we did with students: consistently enforce our high expectations and build a system of support—this time for the teachers—for maximum effectiveness.

Teacher Support

In this era of increased teacher accountability—teachers are expected to raise the performance of all students regardless of socioeconomic status or background—there is a high degree of teacher stress. Quality learning and stressed teachers don't go together. At Granger, we worked hard to support and relieve the stress of our teachers because they were our most valuable asset.

Much of that support came from the systems we implemented. The three-way communication system (see chapter 3) and the advisories (see chapter 4) made our system manageable by effectively enlisting the support of parents and allowing teachers to focus on a handful of at-risk students instead of dozens of vulnerable students. Our English curriculum, which focused on building reading and writing skills (see chapters 5 and 6), reduced the burden of having so many students with low reading skills. Teachers' burdens were further lifted by the systems we put in place that boosted skills and changed student attitudes and beliefs (see chapters 6 and 7).

I was determined to give the teachers everything they needed to be successful, be it technology, supplies, or whatever else they requested. If their needs fit our mission, I wanted to equip them. I didn't want our teachers to feel limited by the budget, to think of the budget as "The Big No." This support meant careful planning and a lot of effort spent seeking additional funds through grants, but it was effort that had a tremendous payoff. People who feel supported will gladly pitch in and be a part of your team.

Another way to support teachers is found in a phrase that Will learned from a colleague of his: we must always remember the dailiness of teaching. This saying means simply that teachers are incredibly busy, constantly surrounded by students and needing to make nonstop decisions, all while being subjected to the tyranny of a bell schedule that stops for no man or woman. Constant interruptions from announcements, students needing notes signed, and students misbehaving—these are the teacher's daily struggles, and all of this dailiness works against implementing new strategies or adding new programs.

By my second year at Granger, we had changed our teaching schedule so that we had two hours set aside every week for professional development. After we looked at data on student performance, we used staff surveys to identify the kinds of professional development our teachers thought they needed. Then we focused on what was either the highest priority or the easiest fit, depending on how much capacity we thought our teachers had for taking on new challenges at that time. From neuroscientists like Earl Miller of MIT, we learn that the brain can focus effectively on only one thing at a time (Hamilton, 2008). As we're busy paying attention to the new, other things can slip out of our control. We see the reality of the continuum of skills acquisition, which says that to really master new skills we go through a process from unconsciously unskilled to consciously unskilled to consciously skilled and finally are able to perform at the level of experts: unconsciously skilled (Gordon Training International, n.d.). It takes time to develop expertise in new strategies and changes in instruction. Supporting teachers means being constantly aware of that development time line and always remembering the dailiness of teaching.

I admire teachers, and I made it a constant practice to connect with them as much as possible, visiting their classrooms throughout the day. I listened carefully to their troubles, and then I did something about those problems. The school-improvement agenda was driven by the plans that we as a school made and then customized to fit what teachers were struggling with as they implemented the plans. When my teachers needed help from the administrative level, they got it. When I saw common threads developing, I connected teachers with each other so that they didn't have to face their issues in isolation.

No substitute exists for this simple strategy of connecting with staff. It's not easy to do when you have a school full of conflict, like the one I faced. Don't give in to the temptation to avoid making contact so that you can avoid unpleasant situations. I can promise you that over time, your efforts will pay off with de-escalating conflict.

High Expectations

I don't think that what I've written in the previous section on supporting teachers would cause teachers to do anything other than cheer. That may not be true
of the next section. Remember the first sentence of chapter 1: this was the angriest school I had ever seen. This was a real school, and this is a real story. There
were teachers at our school who didn't seem to believe that all students could
learn to high standards. There were those who flat-out said we couldn't prepare
a lot of our kids for postsecondary. That was what their experience told them.

When you make bold changes, you face bold challenges, and a leader must be
ready to take on those challenges. You can't turn around your school if even a
few people are acting like anchors, resisting every change. The following sections describe my strategies for pulling up the anchors.

Be Transparent and Consistent

My staff members knew why I held them accountable, because I told them and
I told them often. The message never changed: "We are preparing all our students so that they can have the skills to be successful in postsecondary education
and get training for a good job."

When push comes to shove and shove is winning, reminding people of the goal
is essential. I used our goal like a mantra, repeating it endlessly to get it to sink
in. I also consistently went on to add another important reason: "If we don't help
these students get the skills, we might as well be giving them a lifetime sentence
of poverty." True, we didn't put the students in poverty, but we had the power to
help them climb out of it. If these students didn't get the skills while they were
in school, chances were high that they'd never pick them up, and they would be
stuck repeating the cycle of their parents.

The teachers' responsibility was to encourage and hold students accountable to
state standards. My job was to hold the teachers accountable. We were in this
mission together.

Follow the Union Contract

After I realized just how union-oriented many of my staff members were, I told
them at a faculty meeting that I promised to follow their union contract to
the letter. I had no interest in wasting time fighting grievances, because that
would take energy away from our common mission of getting our kids ready
for postsecondary. I also told them that I was not interested in getting rid of
teachers. According to the contract, dismissal was a two-year process that started
with an improvement-needed evaluation, progressed to providing professional
development and coaching to help the teacher, and then escalated as necessary.

I preferred to work with my teachers to help them grow their skills instead of putting in two years of valuable time to fire them.

The flip side was, of course, that I would hold them to their responsibilities made explicit in the contract. In my mind, there was no room for negotiation. I would do what the contract specified. They would do what the contract specified. I would not deviate. And if they deviated, they faced the consequences spelled out therein. No threats, no intimidation. Just a group of adults agreeing to do what they had agreed to do when they first took the job and signed the contract.

Don't Enter a Fight That You Can't Win

This strategy is closely related to the preceding strategy, and it's the reason I wouldn't go against the contract—it was an unwinnable situation. No one intentionally jumps into a fight knowing he or she can't win. The problem arises when one hasn't done the analysis in advance to keep out of trouble.

If you're going to play a sport or a game, knowing the rules is critical. School leaders—whether superintendent, principal, teacher, or paraeducator—need to know the rules that govern the way the game is played in their arena. For me, this meant that I had to use the teachers' contract as my personal playbook. I have no doubt that I knew it better than any of my teachers, because I studied it when I first started the job and consulted it whenever I had a question. I even carried it with me to staff meetings during that first year. If I needed to make a tough decision or push my staff's comfort zone in some way, I made sure that I was operating by the rules. If I could not get what I wanted by following the rules of the game, I didn't go there.

Beyond the teachers' contract, I studied our state laws regarding education, which in Washington come in the form of WAC (Washington Administrative Code) and RCW (Revised Code of Washington), as well as our school board's policy manual. Believe me when I tell you that all of these manuals are voluminous and that my copies were extensively tabbed and highlighted. It is such a foolish waste of time and energy to try to do the educational equivalent of making a basketball basket worth five points instead of two. Any time spent arguing over impossibilities according to the rules is time that could have been used to educate students.

As a school or classroom leader, you will face fights. Be prepared. Time and again, I have found that everything I really needed to win was already written into law or policy somewhere. It was just a matter of putting the time into studying the rule books carefully.

Go Easy on People, But Be Hard on Standards

Being a member of a sports team can be a magical experience, all hands pulling together toward the same goal, a spirit of unity and trust in one another that makes the losses bearable and the wins so much more gratifying. That's what I wanted for my school: a unified team. The alternative, a team full of infighting and individuals, is not only unrewarding, it's also downright ineffective. If you have to work as a team to accomplish your goals, you can't afford to lose any teammates along the way. But how do you accomplish this while still holding people accountable to high standards?

Instead of face-to-face confrontations, I took the tactic of shoulder-to-shoulder confrontations. Picture two people having an argument. The most contentious position they could be in is a face-to-face confrontation. The problem lies directly between them. The language they use is full of the words *I* and *you*: "Look, you're not following our policy," or "You think I don't know what the policy says? I'm not stupid." Now picture these people turning so that they are standing shoulder to shoulder, facing the same direction. The problem lies not between them; it's out there in front of them. They are not standing on different sides of an issue; they're on the same side of an obstacle, wondering how to get over or around it. They strategize to solve the problem together. The language isn't *you*. It's more like "The standards require us to ..." or "According to the contract, we have to ..." or "What our students need is ..."

I tried to show the staff that I was not the obstacle, nor did I consider them to be obstacles. We had a common enemy to fight, and that was the low performance of our students. For example, when we implemented our mentorship program, some teachers balked at the added responsibility. I could not win this fight by appealing to the union contract. I had to go shoulder to shoulder with my staff and tell them, "Here's the reality of the situation. With a graduation rate of fifty percent, half of our kids are at risk. We are overwhelmed by sheer numbers. In a few short years, our state will require kids to be proficient in reading, writing, and math in order to graduate, which is going to make our problem even worse. I did not make that rule; it's just the way things are. Now my question is, under the circumstances, what can we do to make things different?" With a quick shift in perspectives, we were on the same side of the issue. It didn't mean my staff liked the idea of becoming mentors any more than they had minutes earlier, but they could no longer wholeheartedly believe I was the enemy.

Entrenched Staff

Allow me a few more stories to make crystal clear what I'm talking about when it comes to working with entrenched staff. Remember, none of these struggles were necessary with those who believed in our mission and demonstrated by their actions that they did. However, we had a few teachers who, because of discouragement or fear or force of habit, were actively adversarial. If they did not respond to shoulder-to-shoulder approaches, I had to change tactics. Our mission was too important, and I could not let them sabotage it and the hard work of the other teachers.

The Evaluation Conflagration

After the September rush of events in my first year, I finally had time to turn my attention to instructional leadership. Evidence showed that I had a few veteran teachers who had low expectations of our students and little drive to improve. They had practically laminated their lesson plans from their fourth or fifth year of teaching and had been using them for up to twenty years. Clearly, accurate evaluations were needed to determine what these teachers were doing that was working and what wasn't, and to show them the changes they needed to make to start reaching all their students more effectively.

I announced the upcoming start of evaluations at a faculty meeting, noting that I had to complete two of them for each teacher. One veteran teacher—the union representative for the building—told me, "You know, you have to announce when you're coming into our classrooms for an evaluation." Yes, I agreed, that was true for the first evaluation, but not for the second.

"No, it's in our contract. You have to notify us every time before you come in. That's the rule all our previous administrators went by," said the teacher. I promised the staff that I'd look into the contract. It just didn't sound right to me. After all, what school board would give such limited power to administrators to monitor and improve instruction? Anyone could put on a good show twice a year to demonstrate that they knew what they were doing. We wanted the instruction on the other 178 days to be as good as, or better, than the two evaluation days.

After the meeting, I went straight to my office to read the contract, and I found that it contained no such provision. Just as I thought, one evaluation had to be scheduled and include both a pre- and postevaluation conference. All other evaluations could be based on walkthroughs that accumulated to the required number of observed minutes, and those walkthroughs required no advance notice.

I wrote a memo to the staff that let them know I had looked into the situation. I quoted the relevant part of the contract and restated our goal to remind them what this evaluation period was all about: to help our kids learn the skills to be successful in postsecondary. I agreed with the union contract that the best way to do that was to do unannounced walkthroughs so that I could learn how to support the teachers based on accurate information. Walkthroughs would also help us better reach our goal because we would hold ourselves accountable to the same high standards to which we would hold the students.

At the next staff meeting, I handed out the memo and went over it with the staff. I knew that this was a fight I not only had to win, but also a fight that I was going to win. I'd like to say that I was all smiles as I faced this challenge, but that would be unrealistic. I learned long ago that when someone tries to bully you, you have to stand up to him or her and show no weakness. I didn't need to be nasty or punitive, flinging accusations about being lied to or questioning motives, but I did need to be direct and to the point and have a no-nonsense manner.

Job Description Jousting

By midyear, I was struggling to find the time to get out to the classrooms and do observations because I was always busy putting out fires. It slowly dawned on me that some of those fires might have been deliberately set to keep me from pursuing my agenda. I had an inordinate number of discipline referrals for minor infractions, almost all of them coming from my most entrenched staff members, and they increased dramatically in number after the evaluation conflagration. When I mentioned this to the principal of the middle school, he gave me this piece of advice: "The staff will treat you like gold if you take care of their discipline for them."

I was more interested in treating students' futures like gold and bringing our quality of instruction up to the gold standard. If staff kept flooding me with their responsibilities, we'd never reach that standard. When I pushed them to take care of minor discipline issues in their own classrooms, the pushback was immediate: angry teachers in my office accusing me of lack of support and telling me the whole school was falling apart.

I was keeping in close contact with my superintendent and told him about the issues with which I was dealing. He let me know that he fully supported me and encouraged me to keep up what I termed "quiet and relentless pressure." There was no need to scream and shout and no need to go out of my way to be adversarial, but I had teammates who were not carrying their load, and that had to change.

By this time, I was carrying around the union agreement and our school board policies in a binder. Wherever I went, the binder went, and I started to dig into it to see what it said regarding classroom discipline and the many other small jobs that were finding their way onto my already overloaded plate. As I read the job descriptions written for each position on my staff, including my own, I found written confirmation that my staff was slipping a lot of things onto my plate that they didn't find appetizing.

In keeping with the idea of quiet pressure, I met with each staff member individually and went over job descriptions so that I could make a human connection and head off the mob mentality that sometimes dominated staff meetings. I told each one, "I want to get everyone on the same page. Let's read what your job description says and see if there's anything you don't think should be in there." I was trying to demonstrate that if they did have concerns, we were able to talk about them. In this setting, no one really pushed back, even over the part in the description about the teacher's responsibility for setting up an effective classroom management system.

The only pushback I had was from a counselor who found that her job description said she was responsible for all student testing. She disagreed vehemently because she had never been held responsible for it previously. I could see that taking on the responsibility for testing would be an additional burden, but the alternative was for me to take it on, and that was another thing on my schedule that would keep me out of classrooms and prevent my being a strong instructional leader. So I let her know that from that point forward she would be responsible for testing because, according to the job description, it was part of her job. Her anger flared, and she fired back at me, "Well, maybe I should be looking for another job then."

I had prepared for this kind of reaction from staff. In a calm voice, my tone even and looking her squarely but compassionately in the eyes, I told her that I would be happy to write her a good recommendation if she felt she would be unable to perform the job requirements. Because it was early spring, jobs would soon be opening up, and she should have no problem finding another position. However, I did ask her to take a day to think about it. She left my office in a huff, but when she came back the next day, she apologized for her outburst. I responded by assuring her that I would support her during the transition she would be going through as she took on this new responsibility: "Just keep me in the loop, and let me know what you need."

Getting teachers to be more responsible for classroom management and having the counselor take over our testing program did not revolutionize our school by themselves. But they were small, incremental changes in areas that were making our whole improvement process grind to a halt. Necessary changes in instruction and school climate still waited, but incremental victories in the change process are often necessary to get to the big wins. On the way to the big victories, I was laying the groundwork for teamwork by communicating individually and letting my staff know that I believed in and supported their ability to be successful with our students.

Lesson Plan Procrastination

After the job description jousting, many teachers were not as agreeable as they had been during our individual meetings, and a negative atmosphere was developing. So I called a staff meeting to take the firmest stand yet. First, I passed out photocopies of their union contract, which stated that if a certificated employee knowingly chose to disregard a directive from his immediate superior, that action would be grounds for a serious reprimand or even termination. I looked up from the paper to a roomful of angry faces. "Look," I explained. "I'm not reading this to you as a threat. I'm just responding to the reality of where our working relationship stands currently. I'm here to rally our team so that we can help all our students be successful, but I'm facing a lot of opposition and a lot of negativity. The resistance has to stop. This is about all of our kids learning the skills they need to be successful in postsecondary, so they can go on and have a good job with insurance and a retirement plan, just like the benefits all of you have. I know that your contract gives me the right to get rid of you if you fight me on my directives. But I also know what due process is, and I know that it takes about two years for me to evaluate an unsatisfactory employee out of our school. What a tragic waste of time that would be to take all that time and energy away from our mission of educating students. I don't want to do it. I would much rather work with you to improve our students' skills and test scores than to evaluate you out of a job, but the choice is really yours. Work together or fall—and fail—apart."

I asked for people to speak up and let me know what they thought about my stance. In general, they agreed and said they liked the way I was thinking about it. I again promised them that I would follow the union contract to the letter, both as a way of supporting them and holding them accountable for what was best for our students' success.

That was only the first half of the agenda. The next item dropped on my staff like a bombshell. I told them that from then on, I expected them to turn in monthly unit plans and daily lesson plans that showed how they were making progress toward our state learning goals. You would have thought I had asked for their firstborn children. I asked if they had any questions and received none, but the icy glares were plentiful.

Before they could come to their senses and mount an attack, I dropped the other news. I passed out copies of a few of the RCWs from the *Washington State School Law* book, which stated that teachers were responsible, by law, for timely attendance, grading, and a few other items such as planning. I made it clear that these laws superseded their union contract and that I would follow the RCWs as closely as I followed their contract. I asked for questions, and the room was quiet with a silence that spoke volumes.

I was tested a few times, and I followed through with warnings, so word spread that I meant business. Requiring them to turn in lesson plans was not just game playing or creating busywork. Neither was it a power play where I was trying to show them who was boss. This was an important step in improving instruction: finding out what was really being taught in our classrooms and getting teachers away from laminated lesson plans.

Facing Grievances to Fight for Student Learning

Two additional major issues further set the tone that I meant business. The first incident occurred when I decided not to renew a first-year teacher, one whom the previous principal had hired just before I arrived. This young man was failing 105 out of his 127 students. Whenever I talked to him about it throughout the year, he consistently stated that he was doing his job. It was the kids' fault, according to him. This belief was absolutely unacceptable, a violation of core belief 2, which states that all kids are capable of learning when expected to do so in a positive learning environment. This teacher had not found a way to create that environment; he was negative, and it showed both in his attitude and in the kids' demoralized performance. The union filed a grievance on his behalf, but it was to no avail; probationary teachers had no due process rights under our contract.

The second issue was delivered to me in a sandwich baggie. A central office administrator had seen one of my teachers smoking while standing by his car parked on a side street outside the school. Reminding me of a badly written episode of *CSI*, she threw on my desk a baggie that contained the offending cigarette butt as evidence. As much as this made me want to laugh, I investigated and found that this teacher actually left his classroom unattended, during class, while he went to have a smoke. I called him in for a meeting, during which I gave him a written reprimand. Faster than you can say "nicotine-impaired cognition," he filed a grievance claiming harassment, which, of course, he lost. I was two for two, and my staff knew without a doubt that I not only knew the negotiated contract agreement very well, but also that I would follow through on important breaches of that contract without hesitation.

Core Belief 5

You can't avoid politics, so play the game to win.

Nothing could have trained me better for political battles than being an athletic director. Limited resources (only so many spots on a team, players on the field, minutes in a game) combined with competing interests (my kid needs those resources) result in some pushy—and angry—parents. But it's not just the parents; coaches fight over who gets new uniforms, gym time, and so on.

Fortunately, I got plenty of practice in learning how to balance these competing interests without going crazy.

In my view, the politics of education are extremely similar to the politics of athletics: managing groups and individuals who are competing over limited resources to get what they want. A principal's job is to make sure the decisions he or she makes are good for the whole community and are moving everyone toward the ultimate goal.

Education can be a very serious matter for parents. In some cases, how their child is educated may mean the difference between getting into MIT (Massachusetts Institute of Technology) or not. Other parents count on the school to make sure their child doesn't end up in the welfare office. It all comes down to: what's in it for my child? You probably know it's a bad idea to get between a mama grizzly bear and her cub. The same is true of parents and their children.

I have watched too many people get cut down in political battles and either lose their jobs or lose so much power that they had to resign. People with passion for the cause and brilliant ideas have been lost, and we are poorer because of it. Many never learned that sometimes you have to lose a battle in order to win the war. I've also watched while many good and talented people try to avoid combat altogether, continually placating and soothing. In the end, perhaps they survived, but the mission of turning around their students' learning did not. In order to be successful in turning around a school, principals must play the game of politics well. The following sections describe the strategies I used to deal with angry parents and survive the rough-and-tumble politics that comes with the job.

Deal With Anger

I have learned that sometimes you have to make decisions that will inevitably upset some people. The first step in dealing with anger is acceptance. Accept that if you push change, you will generate some angry responses, and you are powerless to stop it. I've learned not to fear anger, but to expect it, and to maintain a Zen-like acceptance that this is just the way things are. On my desk, I keep a quote from the revered Zen scholar Bill Cosby: "I don't know the secret to success, but the key to failure is trying to please everybody."

The second step in dealing with angry people is to switch from Zen to jujitsu. The benefit of jujitsu is that you learn how to use people's anger-energy against them.

In my view, the main reason to keep your enemies close is not so you can find out what they are up to and do unto them before they do unto you, although in certain political situations you might have to do that. Rather, the meaning of this approach, to me, is that we have to push toward, instead of away from, our enemies.

I learned to view angry people not as enemies, but simply as people who have different opinions. That shift in perspective motivated me to work hard at trying to understand them. I listened. I drew them close to learn about their needs, desires, and fears. These people felt angry for a *reason*, and I wanted them to pour it out. This tactic often defused the anger, showed me what their needs and fears were, and allowed me to identify any mutually satisfying outcomes that presented themselves. I could then redirect the passion of their anger into fulfilling our mission. If given the choice between passionate people who sometimes get angry and passionless people, I'll take the passion any day.

This tactic of pushing toward people's anger also gave them the opportunity to get to know me, not as an enemy, but as someone with a different opinion. I got to repeat the mission and remind them of what we were trying to accomplish. If they couldn't convince me that what they wanted aligned with our mission, well, they could see on my desk the Cosby quote about trying to please everyone. We may have disagreed, and they may have felt angry, but I knew I'd done everything possible to engage them. The only thing left to do was to keep engaging them to try to win them over in time or simply to stop any insubordination immediately.

Make Decisions With Your Own Children in Mind

When it comes to making difficult decisions, I like to keep one thought foremost in my mind, and I teach it to my collaborative decision partners: what would I want for my own kids? For instance, would I want this coach coaching my own children? If not, then it's time to open the position to search for a new coach, which is something I did when I arrived at Granger. I reopened all coaching positions, and incumbent coaches had to reapply and reinterview. This caused no end of complaining, but it gave our interview committee, which was comprised of representatives of the faculty and community, the opportunity to really consider, Is this who I want coaching my kids? We had almost a complete turnover in one year—with excellent results.

When considering current or prospective teachers, ask yourself, Would I want my children in his or her class? If my children needed help with their reading, would I want them in our current reading program? If the answer is no, then it is time to cut programs and work to get teachers reassigned or placed on improvement contracts. Sometimes, it even means overriding committee decisions. This method, of course, is not politically popular, but I'm willing to do battle if I can honestly say I want something for my own kids that is different from the status quo. It is hard to watch people get angry and shed tears, and it is hard to be called names, but it is worse to see students suffer because of bad decisions or because people are afraid to do what's best. I can sleep well at night when I know my decisions are based on this strategy.

Recognize the Difference Between Speed Bumps and Walls

When driving a car, speed bumps can slow down your journey and make it less comfortable, but hitting a wall can damage your car beyond repair and injure or kill you. To lead change, you must know the difference between a speed bump and a wall. Some decisions make for rough riding at times, but others can be fatal to your career and your aspirations. You can't help kids reach their dreams when you've lost your job or your will to fight. This third strategy guides me in knowing when I need to lose a battle in order to win the war.

For example, when our district administration team wanted our school to participate in an employee-of-the-month program, I objected. The research on external motivators is inconclusive at best, but in my view, such programs fall more strongly on the side of being detrimental to morale and divisive to teamwork. I explained my views and recommended that the district abolish the program. My opinions were met with strong resistance.

Thinking this situation would be a speed bump, I requested permission for my building not to participate. But the superintendent was offended by this request, and he stated to me in no uncertain terms that he expected me to be a team player. It was now clear that I was staring at a wall. Did I think my way of doing things would be better? Absolutely. Did I consider simply nominating my whole staff each month as a way to show that we were all a part of making the changes that I anticipated? I'd be lying if I said I didn't. But what good would it do to be stubborn on this point when that was the shortest distance to a headlong crash into a wall? Was the price of being right worth it when it meant I might not be in a position to fulfill my mission, because of a transfer to another position or eventual dismissal?

Remember, It Always Comes Down to a 3–2 Vote

The final authority is the school board, and if you plan to appeal an issue above your supervisor, you had better have the backing of the majority of its members. If not, you will surely hit the wall.

You have to build relationships with some board members, something that is admittedly easier in a smaller district than a large one. In a district of any size, however, you can invite board members to come to your building one at a time. Find out why they wanted to be on the school board and what drives them. Talk about your core beliefs and sell your mission. Talk honestly about the challenges and what you are doing about them. Be ready to answer any questions about contentious issues for which your decisions have angered people. Sell the mission some more.

School board members are not omniscient. If you do not educate them about your school, its challenges, and what you believe are the best courses of action to overcome the challenges, then who will? The small amount of time invested in these activities will produce a large return whenever you face a wall.

Core Belief 6

School improvement must be a team effort.

I used to have a three-legged stool sitting on my desk that had the word *parent* painted on one leg, *student* painted on another, and *educator* painted on the third leg. The round seat on top had the word *responsibility* painted on it. The responsibility of educating students falls on all of us working as a team toward a common goal: preparing students for postsecondary education. Take away one leg, and the whole stool falls. The next chapter focuses on a system that engages parents and encourages them to take on their share of the responsibility. Before getting to that, however, it's important to introduce the concept of the teamwork continuum.

The Teamwork Continuum

Leaders need to always strive to create partners, not adversaries, and to move staff, parents, and students along the teamwork continuum (fig. 2.1) toward the "cooperative" side. The more teammates we create, the easier it is to turn around our schools.

Adversarial   **Cooperative**

Figure 2.1: The teamwork continuum.

Attitude can make all the difference in moving others along the teamwork continuum. Stick to your core beliefs as you encourage others to work with you instead of against you. Restate the goal—to prepare the student for a postsecondary education that leads to the career of his or her choice—and try to move the other person into a shoulder-to-shoulder position on the same side of the issue, looking at how to overcome the common obstacle.

With, Not To

The teamwork continuum is applicable to students, but I have another guiding phrase when it comes to building teamwork with students: "Do with students, not to them." I strongly believe we should involve our students when making decisions that affect their education.

A professor told me about one of her efforts as a high school principal. Her school-improvement team scheduled a group of low-level readers into a new class and implemented a reading intervention program without informing the students. The students followed their printed schedules on the first day of the new grading period, going to a new class with an ambiguous name. Needless to say, it didn't take long for the students to figure out what was happening. As soon as they walked in, they saw all the other kids who were like them, those who were totally disengaged from school and naturally defensive about their lack of success. It didn't matter what the name of the class was. To them, it was English for Stupid People. The class turned into a nightmare because the administrators did this to the students without notifying them and without their consent. The kids didn't like being treated like dummies.

When it comes to motivating students to do the hard work of learning, we must do with them, not to them. We can't force students to work harder than they've worked before. They have to buy into the plan. (Chapters 3, 4, and 6 include strategies to involve students in planning.)

At Granger, I involved students in making decisions about whether they would be suspended or sent to alternative school. We had to make clear to our students who were constantly fighting us that it was their choice of behavior that guided our actions—students participated in getting kicked out of school. The strategies in this book are all based on the principle of not acting as if students are inert objects, but involving them as living, breathing teammates so they will not be our adversaries, but rather our partners.

One Life a Day

One other special strategy for building teamwork bears inclusion here. I think it's one of the most important things a teacher—and especially an administrator—can do. I made a decision to try to touch one life in a meaningful way every day. I didn't always succeed, but I was constantly on the lookout for a ten-minute time slot, whether in my office, in the cafeteria, or at a sporting event, to focus on one student and find out how he or she was doing.

The conversation almost always started out with general inquiries: "Are you having a good day today? What activities are you involved in after school? How is that going?" Then it got more specific: "How are your grades? Which class is giving you the most trouble? What's your reading level? What are you reading at home right now? What's your career goal?" This allowed me to personalize the general messages we were always giving: "Oh, you want to be a veterinarian. How much math do you need for that? How are you doing in math right now?"

Talking one-on-one with students allowed me to connect the present with their future and remind them of the Big W: Work! Anything was possible if only they would do the work: "I don't make the rules of this world, but I sure know what they are. If you want to go to college, you must have four years of math. You may disagree, but it doesn't change what you have to do. So you might as well accept it and get the job done." These conversations allowed me to listen to my students talk about any obstacles that were getting in the way and either give them some advice or talk to my teachers about changes that might help these students.

Core Belief 7

The curriculum must be relevant.

A golden rule for writers and public speakers is to keep their audience in mind when they are communicating. That's good advice for educators as well.

If you are turning around a school, you have students who have been chronically disengaged. At Granger, we made sure to connect the what and why of school to our students. Yes, we still had to have the standard conversations, such as, "You can't always study only stuff that interests you. Sometimes you have to work with information and store it in your head for later when it will make better sense, because learning is like that. We can't predict the future and know exactly everything you'll need, so we can't promise you will need everything, but the process will make you more knowledgeable and help you to learn other things." But we also tried to add, "We'll do our best not to make you go through that too often, but when you're facing it, we need your help to step up and do the learning anyway. Or even better, suggest a better way for us to do it. If you're working with us instead of just complaining, you'll make it a lot easier to say yes to new ideas, and we'll all work together on making your learning more relevant."

We did our part by selecting interventions that worked to make the irrelevant relevant. Reading is boring for those who comprehend poorly and have to work harder than average at it. Our reading intervention had individual, one-on-one conversation time as well as small-group conversation time every day to allow students to make personal connections to what they were reading. Such a connection is one thing that makes reading worthwhile, and for some, these connections while reading were a first-time experience. Are students in your school highly engaged? If not, the relevance of your curriculum to their lives is almost sure to be poorly understood. Of course, relevance is not the only culprit, but it's a major one.

Cultural relevance also has high significance. I will always remember watching a young history teacher at Granger High School teach a unit on the American Revolution. He taught the general concepts of what revolutions are all about, using the American Revolution as the template. Then he gave students the opportunity to research different revolutions that occurred throughout history and present their findings. It was astounding to see the difference in the motivation level between these students and the students who were taught the same unit by a different teacher, motivation stemming from being able to research and present on a topic in which the students were personally interested. The Mexican people alone have many revolutions in their history, and with many students of Mexican descent, that was a popular area of study. The end result was that the students were highly engaged. They learned about the American Revolution and how revolutions in other countries occurred. They were able to go beyond simple comprehension and fact regurgitation to reach levels of comparison and contrast and even analysis. Their understanding of the American Revolution ended up being greater than it otherwise would have been.

Another example, for contrast, was an experience I remember from my high school history class. Our teacher asked us to read about the Mexican-American War and the Alamo. I will never forget my teacher's preparatory lecture about Davy Crockett, Jim Bowie, and 219 other brave souls who stood up to the dictator Santa Anna. They fought bravely before finally succumbing to more than five thousand Mexican soldiers. After the United States was forced into war with Mexico, Sam Houston surprised Santa Anna's army, his men inspired by the battle cry "Remember the Alamo!" as they rode on to victory.

As a teenager of Mexican descent, I felt conflicted. Although I was well liked by most people in my school, I grew up with the feeling that I was looked down on for being Mexican. The Mexican-American War was another example of the Mexicans getting their due. I found it hard to generate any enthusiasm for the assignment. If only my teacher had told me then what I found out years later when I visited the Alamo myself. There in a book in the gift shop, I found the story of Jose Maria "Gregorio" Esparza: a man with my own last name who died as a cannoneer fighting for the American side. Not only that, but Esparza was one of the few killed that day who got a proper burial. His brother, who was fighting for the Mexican army, was allowed to recover his brother's body and inter his brother as befitted his sacrifice and courage.

I'm not suggesting that we completely change our history curriculum for the benefit of some of our students, but imagine this: what would happen if you picked ten random historians and asked them about a historical event? They would each have a different take on the event, and that's pretty good evidence that more than one viewpoint can be considered without taking anything away from the historical record. If opening our curriculum to show students where they fit into the story motivates them to study with more passion, I'd submit that the change, facilitating discussion and negotiation of real-world viewpoints, is far better than our traditional curriculum.

Core Belief 8

You must be data driven from start to finish.

We used our performance data during every step of our school-improvement planning process*es*. (Yes, plural. We started our first at the end of my rookie year and went through another refinement with even more data starting in my fourth year.) Of course, we used all state and district testing data for planning, but when it came to improving instruction, we also used curriculum-based measures such as daily reading improvement in the reading intervention or holistic writing scores based on the state's scoring model. We found that the Measures of Academic Progress (MAP) tests from the Northwest Evaluation Association had a 90 percent correlation to our state assessments, and we used these as well. In addition, we tracked absences and tardies, grades and grade point averages, discipline referrals, graduation rates, reading scores, parent participation in conferences, and the number of books read, both per student and for the whole school.

All of the data we tracked became fodder for communication. We talked about troubling data in newsletters. We displayed numeric improvement goals on posters. We cheered about successes in PowerPoint presentations to the students, the staff, and the school board. Data that stay in spreadsheets and notebooks are not truly owned. So choose relevant data, communicate those data to all parties, set targets for improvement, and share the results of new efforts. The process works only when the data becomes public.

communication

Will All of This Really Work?

Granger High School provided me with the opportunity to prove that what I believed would really work. If I could not prove that it could be done, I knew that I was still young enough to leave the profession and try something new. That's how serious I was about helping to turn around this school. In my previous school, I had worked hard to change things from the curriculum side, but even as I saw improvements in that area, I still saw all the pain and suffering and the fighting and yelling among students, parents, and teachers. Why wasn't what we were doing in that school working? Was it even possible to change all this solely by focusing on the curriculum? I spent considerable time reflecting on my own life and decided that the reasons for my own personal success, my climb from poverty to principal, had a lot more to do with human factors than curriculum factors. The next chapter explores just what I learned.

Chapter 3

PARENT ENGAGEMENT STRATEGIES

Some tragedies are so momentous that we can never forget where we were and what we were doing when they occurred. I was standing in the cafeteria doing lunch duty during the spring of my first year as principal at Granger High School when I had one of those moments: an experience that shook me to the core and changed everything from that moment forward. This chapter is dedicated to the mother of four children who opened my eyes to just how important communication is to our educational system.

I'd like to say that I was just standing in the cafeteria watching the remaining students happily shuffle off to class, but in truth, I was actually doling out the extra encouragement that so many of the students still needed to get moving in the right direction. Out of the corner of my eye, I saw storm clouds brewing: a parent approaching, visibly upset. Being the principal of an at-risk high school for almost a year had prepared me to expect the worst. By this point, I had been yelled at by the best.

The parent was a middle-aged woman who addressed me sharply: "Mr. Esparza, I need to speak to you right now regarding the suspension of my son!" We were hardly in an optimal environment for a private and productive conversation. I replied that I would be happy to schedule an appointment as soon as I finished supervising the lunch session. Without hesitation, she responded, "Mr. Esparza, I need to talk to you right NOW because I need you to let my son back into school so that he can graduate!"

It was clear that this conversation was going to happen on her terms, so I motioned for her to follow me to a corner of the room a little farther away from the students who wanted to see the principal get a dose of Mrs. Cordoba. As we walked the few steps to the corner, my mind quickly reviewed her son's case. Her son had committed a disciplinary infraction severe enough that I had to suspend him for three days. He was supposed to be finishing his senior year, but when I looked up his credit record before suspending him, I found that he was seriously deficient in core academic credits. What was surprising was that Mrs. Cordoba didn't know this. We held parent conferences every year and sent home progress reports at regular intervals. We mailed a letter, in English and Spanish, to the home of every senior who was in danger of not graduating, which, unfortunately, was a considerable number. Obviously, her son had scrambled like a pro cornerback to intercept these warnings before the communication was completed. It was also clear that Mrs. Cordoba had not attended our conferences a few weeks earlier.

My mind worked furiously to find an easy way to break the bad news to this parent. She was plenty angry, but that anger told truth to the lie that many staff members believed about her. They thought she was a woman who didn't really care about how her kids did in school. But I saw in a flash that they were completely wrong. If this mother didn't care, she wouldn't be here now or be stating her case so forcefully. Realizing this and finding no magic words that would make everything better, I decided to give the news to her in a straightforward manner.

"Mrs. Cordoba, I'm sorry to be the one to have to inform you, but your son is not going to graduate this year. He has earned only six credits in the last four years here at Granger High School. He needs twenty-one credits to graduate. He also needs to have a lot of credits in our core classes of English, math, social studies, and science, but all six of his credits have been in physical education and vocational electives. Even if I let him back into school today, there is no way he will graduate this year. In fact, because he is so far behind in his credits, he would not even be able to graduate if he came back to school next year and did an extra year of school. He's just too far behind."

Mrs. Cordoba stood there, her mouth slightly open, shell-shocked. I had just witnessed the death of a dream.

After a few silent moments, big tears welled up in her eyes. "Mr. Esparza, that is not possible. I have fed him breakfast for four years and given him lunch money every day so that he would graduate. My son promised me he would graduate and get a good job so he could help me at home. I have no husband and three more children to take care of. If he doesn't get a good job, I don't know what we'll do. Please, Mr. Esparza, please find a way to help my son graduate," she pleaded.

What could I do? I walked her to the counseling department and tried to console her on the way. I told her about a general equivalency diploma program that her son could enroll in to help them move forward with his education. I walked away numbly, my legs somehow finding my way to my office, where I sat for some time behind my closed door wondering what had happened for things to have gone so horribly, horribly wrong.

What's Wrong With That Mom?

I told that story to an interviewer from an educational website, and the response from some of his readers, themselves parents, was striking. What's wrong with that mom? How could she have been so out of touch with reality? Surely this kind of parent is a black swan, an occurrence so far outside the norm that you could never predict it, let alone know what to do when you actually encounter it. These readers, who had a high enough level of education to be interested in and able to read an education-themed website, were very different kinds of parents from Mrs. Cordoba. They could not begin to relate to or even understand her predicament. They wrote comments attacking this woman, whose shoes they had never walked in, with vehemence and disbelief. They blamed the parent.

The response from educators at conferences is different: knowing nods of agreement sweep the room. Behind every nod, I know there is another story of another parent not all that different from Mrs. Cordoba. The educators know that she is not a black swan. Their hearts have broken over parents like her—or at least, their hearts used to break. Many educators inevitably wear down after years of failed efforts trying to engage parents. In the end, some of these educators come to the same place as the people who read my interview on the web: they blame the parents.

It's Not Because She Didn't Care

To my frustrated colleagues, I have two things to say. First, blaming the parents will not solve the problem. Second, the problem is not that uninvolved parents don't care; it's that caring parents are uninvolved. I have never met a single parent in twenty-seven years of education who really wanted his or her child to fail in school.

Mrs. Cordoba is an extreme example of a parent who seemed apathetic and uncaring. But listen to her words. Look at the reasons she had to care. She was desperate for her son to receive an education so he could work to help them improve their lives. Every day, she did her best. She fixed her son a good breakfast, gave him lunch money, and sent him to school. The problem was not lack of effort; it was lack of knowledge. In her mind, fixing him breakfast and making sure he had a good lunch was enough. She didn't understand that she needed to follow her son's education and communicate with him to ensure that he stayed on track.

This is good news! Lack of knowledge and misinformation are things schools are designed to deal with. We educate people. Why would we think our ability to do so ends somewhere after we've taught them to be responsible with driving and voting but before we're sure they can be responsible with drinking?

We *can* educate parents. In fact, we *must* educate them if their ignorance is part of the problem.

But how could this mother not have known she needed to track her kid? How could she have been so blind? How could she have spent so much time and effort focusing on the wrong things? Consider two things: where her ignorance came from and a couple of blind spots of our own.

It's in Our Educational Blind Spot

First, let's look at our own blind spots. Most educators are aware of the phrase "rigor, relevance, relationships," which was the catchphrase of a movement for school redesign. A lot of intelligent people worked on developing the framework for that movement, and many individuals still do. I think the concepts are brilliant. If we develop curriculum that is challenging and rigorous and make it relevant both to students and to the world in which they will have to work in the 21st century, we will be preparing them to compete in a global economy. If we build strong relationships with our students, they will feel nurtured and supported enough to do the hard work of the rigorous learning we're asking of them. It sounds like a perfectly designed system for success, but it's not foolproof.

Buried in the assumptions of this model is a concept equally as important as rigor, relevance, and relationships. This unspoken element is responsibility, and it needs to be added to the other three elements. Without students taking the responsibility to pay attention when they don't feel like it, to finish their homework when they'd rather be on Facebook, or to choose to behave sensibly when confronted by the thousands of moment-by-moment decisions they face daily, there is no assurance that redesigning a school for rigor, relevance, and relationships will have the desired outcome. We can and have expended a tremendous amount of energy on school-improvement movements that forget some very important things.

Another of our blind spots is found in the small-schools movement, an effort to make high schools work better by making them smaller and more personal. The smaller school makes it possible for teachers, students, and administrators to get to know each other better, to develop better relationships that support better learning. In theory it sounds wonderful, but smallness itself is no guarantee of success, and relationships do not magically improve when you have fewer bodies in the room. When I arrived at Granger, it was already a small school, and it was failing miserably with strained relationships among students and teachers.

We can—and do—spend extraordinary amounts of time restructuring a curriculum, a schedule, or even a whole school, all with the best intentions. We can't merely *hope* that productive, responsibility-enhancing relationships will develop simply by changing the structure. Instead, we have to put mechanisms in place to grow the kind of relationships we need. The system explained in this chapter has the mechanisms in place to develop both relationships and responsibility.

In light of these two examples of institutional blind spots, where we as educators put the emphasis on the wrong things, it might be easier to be empathetic toward Mrs. Cordoba's blind spot. But where did her misunderstanding originate?

It's the Poverty

It would be easy and mostly accurate to point the finger at poverty. Sociologists Sara Lawrence-Lightfoot and Annette Lareau have observed that parents who are poor tend to interact with their children and their children's schools differently from middle- and upper-class parents. Lawrence-Lightfoot (2003) points out that poor parents "feel uncomfortable coming to school or approaching their child's teacher … have no idea how to negotiate the institutional bureaucracy, and … tend to see the teacher as the ultimate authority and rarely question her judgment" (p. 109). In dealing with teachers, poor parents are more "withdrawn, uncomfortable, and passive" (Lawrence-Lightfoot, 2003, p. 109) than affluent parents. Lareau tells of her observation of a low-income parent who attended a parent conference. When told that her son had not been turning in homework, the mother was surprised, but all she said was, "He did it at home" (Lareau, 2003, p. 157). There was no follow-up or negotiation with the teacher or other problem-solving behavior. It is as if the mother believed, Lareau said, "it is up to the teachers to manage her son's education. That is their job, not hers" (p. 157).

I don't think that lower-SES parents believe it's not their job to manage their kids' education as much as they think that the schools are in a better position to do it than they are. The parents don't believe they have the skill sets to help in the process of educating their children, so they defer to the professionals. But the end result is the same one that Lareau identifies. In a society where schools are set up to do the teaching and teachers expect parents to make sure their kids are paying attention and doing their work, many parents are throwing the system out of balance. Parents like those cited by these researchers are not doing what we need them to do.

I stated earlier that it is "mostly accurate" to blame poverty for this kind of disengaged parenting for two reasons. First, these behaviors are not always limited to low-income parents. Whether it is overly busy parents who default to the schools, families with significant disruptions in their relationships who don't have the emotional energy to be involved, or just a cultural shift over time toward letting schools take care of the ever more complex business of schooling, the problem is more than just uninvolved poor parents. Second, poverty can't take the sole blame because there are poor parents who do track their kids. In fact, I'm very well acquainted with one particular set: my own parents.

My parents were like Mrs. Cordoba in many ways. They were farm workers, and they were poor. Their office was an asparagus field in the early spring; cherry, peach, and pear orchards in the summer; and apple orchards and grape vineyards in the fall. I may not have known how to hold a pencil before my first day of kindergarten, but I knew how to wield an asparagus-cutting knife. My parents repeated a cycle of poverty they inherited from their parents. Neither my dad nor my mom made it past the third grade because they had to work in the fields to support the family. And yet, they raised a son who not only graduated from high school, but also went on to get his bachelor of arts degree, then a master of science degree, and even his administrative credentials in education.

I knew that poverty could be overcome, even as I sat in my darkened office shortly after leaving Mrs. Cordoba with the counselor. What I didn't recognize were the differences between Mrs. Cordoba and my parents. I didn't see what my parents had done that was so uncharacteristic of many other lower-SES parents. All I could see was that I had turned out so differently from what Mrs. Cordoba's son was turning into. On that painful day, my heavy heart made analysis difficult, but it made resolve easy. I vowed that never again would I let Granger High School be the place where dreams go to die.

Over the days and weeks that followed, I continued to ponder the problem. I didn't yet know the work of Lareau and Lawrence-Lightfoot, so I found myself analyzing what I did know: my own story. Somewhere in it had to be the answer to why I was able to use education to lift myself out of poverty. I didn't want easy answers; I wanted the truth, because only the truth would be powerful enough to prevent other students from going the way of young Mr. Cordoba. That's when I realized that something about my parents must have been different.

The Question That Unlocked the Answer

What did my parents do that helped me to escape the cycle of poverty? Eventually I had an aha moment.

My parents believed in hard work, something they constantly communicated to my four siblings and me. No one knows better than the poor that you can't get anywhere in life without hard work. Like Mrs. Cordoba, my parents didn't have the experience to understand a lot about the way the school system worked. But unlike Mrs. Cordoba, my parents understood one thing very well: the difference between an A and an F.

I'm being completely serious here. As we began to implement the student-led conferences that grew out of my encounter with Mrs. Cordoba, we noticed that some parents smiled and nodded as their child showed them a report card full of Fs. It's possible that the students were telling them in Spanish that an F stood for "fantástico," but whatever story the students told, we had to intervene to explain that an F is not a good thing. Many of our parents had no experience with the American school system, and things we assumed they knew, they just didn't know.

My parents, on the other hand, knew that an F was bad, an A was good, and that you had to work hard to get one but not the other. If you had a grade other than an A, it meant that you weren't working hard. Why should you get to go to school and laze around when they were out working hard in the fields? Working hard was expected, and if you weren't going to work hard in school for the teachers, then you were coming to the fields to work hard for them. I knew they meant it. Out in the fields, they could measure how hard I worked by how long it took me to get to the end of an asparagus row. Measuring how well I was doing in school became just as simple.

My parents also knew that getting As meant that you could get a good job later, one that paid more money than working in the fields, one that would not break your back and make you old before your time. Mrs. Cordoba also saw the value of education, but she thought that graduating was the key to success. Not only did she not understand what was needed in order for her son to graduate, but also she was misinformed. Simply graduating was not enough to guarantee success, not if her son hadn't done the hard work to develop the skills that would allow him to enroll in postsecondary schooling. Without the advanced skills, there would be no advanced training. And without the advanced training, there would be no good job.

So what was the secret to my parents' success in raising my siblings and me to go on to postsecondary education and break the poverty cycle? The following short list includes their simple secrets:

- They believed in and enforced hard work and responsibility.
- They knew how the grading system worked and that they wanted us to earn good grades.
- They kept track of our performance to find out whether we were working hard at school.

Was that it? Could it be so simple?

Yes. My parents didn't have to show up at career day at school or help us with homework, things they could not do anyway. They simply knew when the report cards were due to come home, and they let us know what the report cards were supposed to show (and "fantástico" was not on the acceptable list).

This aha moment made me realize that I needed to find a way to replicate the same basic communication system my parents used: basic but powerful beyond measure due to its simplicity.

The Old Communication System

When I looked at the communication system at Granger, it was easy to see why it wasn't working. What we were doing was pretty similar to what most high schools have traditionally done: use the progress report system.

The Progress Report System

Granger High School was on a semester grading system with two semesters per year, broken up into four quarters. The only grades that went on students' permanent transcripts were the semester grades; the "report cards" for the quarters were really more like progress reports that let students and parents know how the kids were performing. Like many schools, we didn't want to wait until the end of the quarter because students could get dangerously off track in nine weeks. So, at the halfway point of the first quarter, after just four weeks of school, we prepared progress reports and sent them home with the students. Four to five weeks later, we mailed the first-quarter report card. We repeated this the next quarter so that students and their parents had three formal opportunities to learn how the students were doing and respond while there was still time for students to improve their grades. The whole process repeated for the second semester.

We put a lot of time into communicating, but we weren't getting the results we wanted. In the case of Mrs. Cordoba's son, we communicated directly with him about his progress when we talked to him at school. We put progress reports in his hands and asked him to deliver them to his mother and return them with her signature. In that way, we hoped to communicate with her. We thought we were directly communicating with Mrs. Cordoba when we mailed home the quarter and semester report cards. At the time, we wanted our communication system to look like the one shown in figure 3.1.

In this communication process, we talked to the student about his or her performance at school, we sent reports home to the parent, and we hoped the student and parent would talk about how school was going and decide on what, if any, action to take. This is what the traditional reporting system in most schools looked like. That system may have worked fine in some schools or in years past, but it clearly wasn't working for us.

In the case of Mrs. Cordoba and her son, the communication process looked more like the one shown in figure 3.2. No one from the school really knew what Mrs. Cordoba's son was communicating to her.

What could we have done differently? Phone calls from the teachers? Our teachers often tried to call parents, only to become discouraged. Usually, teachers could not reach the parents during the day because the parents were at work. The lower-SES parents didn't use answering machines, and the poorest parents didn't

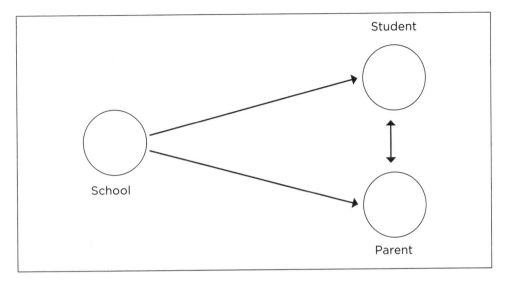

Figure 3.1: How we wanted our communication to look.

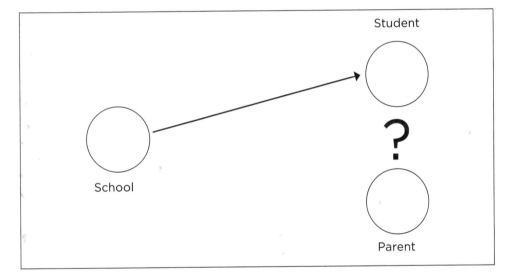

Figure 3.2: How our communication actually looked.

even have phones. If teachers were able to reach them at all, the parents' language differences often hampered communication. When teachers were able to leave a message with a child who answered the phone, the call was rarely returned. The telephone was clearly not a good solution.

The Conference System

In addition to sending home progress reports and attempting phone calls, we held an open house in the fall and parent conferences in the spring. The open house was mostly traditional in the sense that we invited parents to come to the school to meet their children's teachers. It was also traditional in the sense that, like most high schools' open houses, attendance was sparse.

During the spring conferences, parents could ask teachers how their children were doing and talk about which classes they should take the next year. We set up these conferences arena-style in the gymnasium, with tables or desks, one per teacher, placed in a huge circle. The teachers, armed with their gradebooks and progress reports, sat on the outside of the circle facing in, and parents were invited into the middle of the circle. From there, parents could wander to any of their children's teachers.

After seeing the low turnout for the fall open house that first year, I asked my staff if attendance got any better for the spring conferences. They told me that only about 10 percent of the parents attended the conferences. I was a coach for many years, and I knew the difference between a 9–1 (wins–losses) and a 1–9 season. My school was 1–9, and the morale showed it.

I simply could not accept only 10 percent of our parents showing up, so for the spring conferences held during my first year, we made two important changes. First, we visited five hundred homes in our district in hopes of reaching all our students' families. If companies with products to sell could send salespeople door-to-door instead of waiting for customers to come to them, why couldn't we do the same? We organized volunteers into teams consisting of staff members and a student, and sent them out into the community after school to visit parents. At each door, we introduced ourselves, provided some literature in English and Spanish about the important initiatives going on at our school, and invited the parents to visit us at school to see what we were doing. We also asked parents if they had any questions or concerns about the school. In essence, we rolled out the welcome mat.

Second, we moved our conferences, which were held during school hours, to both afternoon and evening hours. Our districtwide conference week schedule ran from Monday to Thursday with the kids released at lunch and conferences scheduled for the afternoons. How many parents could not attend because of work? I told the teachers they would have to meet with parents at the parents' convenience, not their own.

How did I get the teachers, and their union, to agree to this scheduling change? It was actually pretty simple. We did a time swap, as shown in table 3.1. As an added bonus, the new conference schedule was actually three hours shorter and ended one day earlier in order to compensate the staff for having to come back to school in the evenings.

Table 3.1: The Conference Schedule Change

Original Conference Schedule	New Conference Schedule
Monday 12 p.m.–3 p.m.	Monday 5 p.m.–8 p.m.
Tuesday 12 p.m.–3 p.m.	Tuesday 12 p.m.–3 p.m.
Wednesday 12 p.m.–3 p.m.	Wednesday 5 p.m.–8 p.m.
Thursday 12 p.m.–3 p.m.	No conferences

During the first night, I was struck by how impersonal the conferences were. A few parents would straggle in and stand in line to talk to a particular teacher. A piece of tape on the floor in front of each teacher kept parents from getting too close while a teacher was talking to another parent, but of course, anyone waiting in line could still hear much of what the teacher was saying. I remember thinking that a person actually had more privacy filling a prescription at a pharmacy than these parents had while talking to an educator about their children's future.

Very little could actually be accomplished during a five-minute conference, which is all the time we allocated to each parent for each teacher. After all, each teacher at Granger had 100–180 students, so we could not give every parent an unlimited amount of time. Compounding matters, the kids who were doing poorly were no dummies when it came to dodging trouble. None of them came to the conferences with their parents, which made it even more difficult to identify the sources of students' troubles.

At one point, a parent who spoke only Spanish walked in. The instructional assistant who was helping at the door yelled across the gym, "Translator! Translator needed!" Heads of parents waiting in line all swiveled to see what the commotion was all about, and the Spanish-speaking parent looked completely stunned, with her eyes wide open. Fortunately, she ignored the unfriendly and culturally insensitive welcome and visited all seven of her son's teachers. I later learned that she was told seven times that her son was not only failing, but also that he was a discipline problem in class. The good news was that this parent learned about the problems her son was having. The bad news was that there was no way she had enough time with the teachers to figure out a practical, in-depth plan for what she could do to turn him around.

It's not hard to imagine that her son had a pretty rough night after she returned home, but did the conference make a difference? I don't remember hearing about any miracle student turnarounds that first year, so probably not. The arena-style conferences we had with his mother looked like the communication system shown in figure 3.3 (page 44).

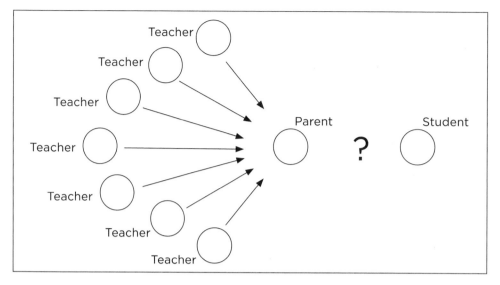

Figure 3.3: How the communication of our arena-style conferences looked.

Talk about target practice! No wonder our past attendance rate was only 10 percent.

After conference week, I sat down to run the numbers, and after all the work we did, we managed to persuade just 27 percent of our parents to attend. My staff was delighted. I had to admit that this number was an improvement, but the coach in me knew we had gone from being 1–9 to only being 3–7. There was not a lot to cheer about. We needed a system with mechanisms built in that ensured our parents would become more engaged, not a system that just offered them opportunities.

Changing the Communication System

Right about the same time as our failed conferences, I met an experienced administrator from our local educational service district (ESD). In Washington, nine ESDs functioned like co-ops, providing experts to schools who otherwise could not afford them. The administrator offered to help me steer a school-improvement process, and I jumped at the chance. As we started the planning process, I thought about how to reach all the parents, such as Mrs. Cordoba, and teach them to do what my own parents had done. Over time, a brand-new system of communication started to form in my mind. The pyramid shown in figure 3.4 conceptualizes this new communication system.

A Student-Centered Approach

Notice the position of the student in the pyramid shown in figure 3.4. The communications and efforts of this new system had a clear focus; this communication

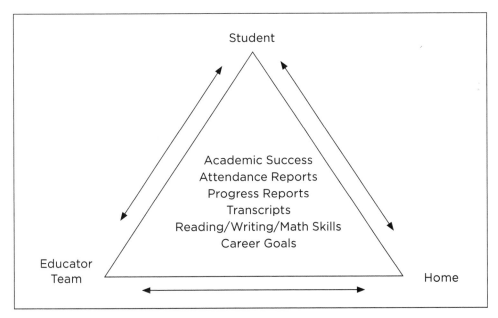

Figure 3.4: The communication power pyramid.

system was all about what students needed, and needed to do, in order to climb as high as they could. We wanted to build better teamwork between school and home so that both could better support students in doing their jobs of learning. The shape of the pyramid, of course, represented that strong foundation of support that enabled students to build ever higher.

The Building Blocks of Success

The center of the pyramid contained the building blocks of student success. To ensure academic success, these were the elements that we needed to monitor:

- **Academic success.** Once again, we ultimately wanted our students to be academically successful, so they would have the best possible chance of leading successful and productive lives.

- **Attendance reports and current progress reports.** Current grades and attendance reports focused on what was happening in classes now. They were the elements that were most amenable to immediate change and where immediate results could be seen.

- **Transcripts.** Transcripts showed whether students were on track for graduation and whether they were taking the kinds of classes that would prepare them for their career choices. The transcripts focused on what had been accomplished—or not—in the past.

- **Reading/writing/math skills.** Were students keeping up with grade-level expectations in these core skills areas? If not, all parties needed to know that and plan and initiate appropriate interventions. Otherwise, students' progress toward their career goals and future success was in jeopardy.

- **Career goals**. Career goals are not just for the future; they also motivate current efforts. Some students initially had very vague career goals, such as, "I don't want to work in the fields like my parents," but over time, we used discussions with the students and their parents to motivate students to more clearly identify the kind of future for which they wanted to prepare.

Many middle- and upper-class parents routinely manage these building blocks with their children—talking about them, planning with them, and intervening as necessary. Not so with many lower-SES parents. We designed our system to teach parents of poverty how to do what middle-class parents already knew how to do.

The Importance of Dialogue

Parent engagement experts often talk about two-way communication, referring to the back-and-forth dialogue needed between home and school. In our old systems, we were guilty of talking *to* parents, not talking *with* them. We told parents, "This is the way things are with your student, and this is what you need to do." We still needed to talk about those elements in the center of our pyramid, but we also needed to support parents by helping them deal with the obstacles they faced. That meant asking what was getting in the way of getting the job done and listening to their responses. If we could understand what their obstacles were, we could help them figure out a way to get around them, or better yet, let them figure out a way. Simply by asking the question, we could be the catalyst for parents to solve problems, coming up with solutions that fit their family style, needs, and schedule. In my experience, when people come up with their own solutions, they are much more likely to implement them, so this kind of two-way communication would be far superior to the old-style, one-way communication.

Three-Way Communication Is Better Than Two-Way Communication

Our model needed to go beyond supportive two-way communication with the parents, however. I thought it was better to create three-way communication, as the arrows in figure 3.4 (page 45) show. The students were the ones who actually had to do the climbing and face the obstacles. Whether the obstacles were of their own creation or created by others, we needed to have a dialogue with them about what was holding them back.

Anyone who teaches high school or middle school, or who has children of that age, knows that having productive conversations with teens is not always easy. In many homes, communication about school and future all but ceases as teenagers go through the developmental stage of separating from their parents. Because of this challenge, our model needed to have the advantage of opening up communication not only between teachers and students, but also between parents and students. This three-way communication would be a mechanism to ensure that these important conversations were taking place and that there was input from all three parties.

Everyone would be clear about what work needed to be done and who needed to do what, and each party would commit to doing his or her part. We could not allow conversations about students' futures, and what they were doing in the present to prepare for them, to get buried in the I-don't-want-to-talk-about-it phase of adolescence. We needed to bring up the subject and get all involved parties in agreement.

The Unavoidable Second Pyramid

At this juncture, a touchy subject came up, one many of us would have liked to avoid. When we asked parents and students to talk with us about what obstacles they faced, we had to be ready to deal with a second pyramid, as shown in figure 3.5.

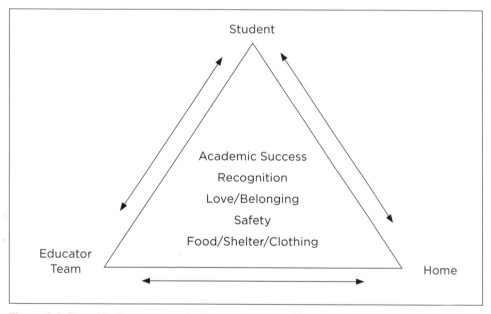

Figure 3.5: The affective communication power pyramid.

Abraham Maslow (1954), a twentieth-century American psychologist, was famous for his "hierarchy of needs." In order for humans to reach their highest potential, their needs—from the most basic survival needs up through more complex sociological and psychological needs—have to be met. The center of our second pyramid paraphrases the needs Maslow identified.

For students whose basic needs are not being met, just talking about transcripts is not enough to help them succeed academically. At every moment, students are affected by forces that are out of their control, forces that make paying attention in school or believing they can bring up their reading level difficult, if not impossible. These issues are the out-of-school factors that researchers point to when they say that schools cannot act alone to improve impoverished students' educations.

But I'm not talking about schools acting alone. I'm talking about schools partnering with parents and students and then acting all together to solve the seemingly intractable problems, one student and one problem at a time. As anthropologist Margaret Mead said, "Never doubt that a small group of thoughtful, committed citizens can change the world. Indeed, it is the only thing that ever has." In the system we designed, *we*—educators, parents, and students—could be that small, thoughtful group.

Why Educator Teams Are Necessary

In our communication system, we used the term *educator team*, not *teacher*. As I talked to our teachers about my vision for a new communication system, several of them responded with "I'm not a counselor!" or "I'm not a social worker!" I could not agree with them more. Caring about students' physical, emotional, and social needs is one thing; having the competence to meet those needs is another. Because teachers are not trained to be counselors and social workers, I did not want them to take on that role, at least not fully. As laypersons, our teachers could handle many of the issues that students brought to them. Encouragement or sharing from their own experiences with the student, even becoming more sensitive to a particular issue a student faced and making accommodations for him or her—these are strategies that teachers employ all the time when they become aware of the needs. But when our teachers reached the limits of their knowledge, experience, or competence level, I wanted them to team with other trained professionals to form an educator team.

Like many schools in impoverished areas, we applied for grants that helped us with social service issues. In addition to our traditional school counselor, we had either on our staff or readily available to us a whole team of social service professionals. We had a drug and alcohol intervention specialist. A parent outreach coordinator connected families to area services such as food banks, domestic abuse shelters, counseling, and medical services. A community grant paid for a police officer to work closely with our school. We even had a home visitor who traveled to households without phones and made contact with students' families.

We informed our teachers about the help these professionals could provide so that they would make use of the available services when necessary. I wanted our three-way communication system to become a referral mechanism to get students and their families the help they needed. It would all start with the teacher, but it wouldn't stop there as the pros worked to do what they could to help our students.

Home Is Where the Help Is

In our communication system, the term *home* represented any adult who cared about and was committed to the student. Some students' parents were not able or available to be involved in supporting their children. Some students lived with grandparents, aunts and uncles, or older brothers and sisters. Some kids were staying with a friend because they had been kicked out of their own houses, and their friend's parent came to conferences with them. A few of my students had neighbors or people from church come.

We could not mandate what "home" was for our students. The important thing was to have at least one adult who was committed to each student. That was the person we wanted to talk with and invite into this powerful three-way communication for ensuring each student's academic success.

The Bottom Line

To ensure that all students reached their potential, we needed all three parties—educator team, home, and students—to agree on student skill sets in reading, writing, and math. The three would have honest discussions about where students were and about the interventions needed to get students where they wanted to go. Then the educator teams, caregivers (home), and students would agree on which responsibilities each would take on in order to accomplish the goal.

The Implementation of Our New Communication System

We took the following steps to begin making the communication pyramid a reality:

1. We reduced the teacher-student ratio to 1:20 and made each teacher responsible for 20 students, not 150 (see chapter 4 for details).

2. We set personal appointments with parents and students to discuss student performance.

3. We increased the duration of conferences from five minutes to thirty minutes.

Our teachers had been each responsible for a load of 150 students. Because those numbers make it impossible to connect well with all those students, let alone their parents, we changed our schedule at the start of my second year to include an advisory period. All teachers taught an advisory, which consisted of approximately eighteen to twenty students. I taught one, too. Because an advisor would keep the same students every year as they moved through our school, this became the perfect vehicle for moving forward with our three-way communication system. Advisors would now be responsible for getting to know their twenty students and for knowing how they were doing in school, as well as their current skill levels in reading, writing, and math—the big three.

Our advisors began making personal appointments with each student and his or her parents to sit down and go over the student's performance, instead of using our arena conferences for communication. We held these appointments in the fall, early enough to catch any problems before students got too far behind with their work, and again in the spring. The appointment in the spring replaced the old arena conferences. Individual conferences were much more effective than sending parents into the arena. We still held our open house in the fall, though, frankly, I didn't think it had much impact on student learning, especially compared to the individual conferences held a month or so later.

I told students that these appointments were just like going to the dentist every six months for a checkup. If checking up on their dental health was important, how much more important was it to check up on their academic health? This new system enabled students to take any necessary corrective action immediately, preventing bigger, more expensive problems later.

How did we schedule teachers for this? Like we did in our move to hold some conferences in the evening (see table 3.1 on page 43), we traded time for time with the teachers. We gave our teachers the freedom to hold all of their conferences during the day if that's when the parents could attend. They could work long days into the evenings on Monday and Tuesday and get all of their appointments done for the week if that plan fit everyone's schedules. Or they could spread out conferences throughout the week. Flexible scheduling was key to making this work. (The appendix at the end of this book includes a reproducible copy of the letter we sent home for our first conference in the spring of 2001; see page 182. Visit go.solution-tree.com/schoolimprovement to download the reproducibles in this book.)

Our conferences did not necessarily end when the clock and calendar said they were finished. I encouraged teachers to reschedule conferences that were missed, so in the weeks after conference week, we still had parents coming in. The window was not closed; we kept on going. Peer pressure started to build among the teachers to get all of their parents to come in for a conference as more and more teachers used that extra time and then bragged when they reached 100 percent. That pressure would not have existed had we let the calendar indicate when the conferences were over. The end result was that some of our teachers actually started making home visits in order to reach the parents of all their students. I can tell you with a high degree of certainty that this never happened under our old conference system!

We scheduled each conference, or appointment, to last thirty minutes and take place in the advisor's classroom. Typically the student, parents or caregivers, and advisor all sat around a table or faced each other at desks that were pulled together. Sometimes whole families attended together, and we welcomed them.

offer child care?

Agendas

We worked from an agenda to keep the conference focused on what was important. This agenda changed over time as we learned how to use our new system better. Before the conference week, we went over the agendas with the staff during our weekly professional development time.

Figure 3.6 shows a sample agenda from one of our first conferences under the new system.

1. Smile (universal language).
2. Explain purpose of meeting (to establish partnership with parents/student to develop a career plan for student success).
3. Review the following:
   - Informational flyer about how our school is organized
   - Credits earned and the importance of student's mastery of skills for graduation and career opportunities
   - Attendance and how important it is for academic success and career opportunities
   - Progress reports: let parents know that teachers are available before and after school if they need more information
   - Interest inventory / career pathway, possible career choices: emphasize that student will be able to change career options at any time
   - Remind parents/student that all careers require good academic skills
4. Review the personalized education plan.
5. Conclusion. Thank them for coming and ask if there are any final questions. **Inform parents of next meeting date.**

Figure 3.6: Agenda for parent conferences.

Welcome Activities

Ninety-five percent of our staff was white and came from a middle-class background. Ninety percent of our students were of color and poor. In a color-blind society, this disparity doesn't make any difference. But in the real world, it makes a lot of difference, not because of skin color, but because of culture.

If a fish were able to talk, what do you think it would say when you asked it to describe water? I imagine it would reply, "What water?" The fish never thinks about water, even though water affects every moment of its life. That is what culture is like. Culture is something that invisibly surrounds us as we grow up. It is the way others around us act and talk and react to everyday situations. In our minds, it is just the way things are, and we pick up an unconscious knowledge of how things are done and what they mean. We absorb the meaning of body language and gestures, tone and volume of voice, and how people around us act in different situations and different roles. If people do not look us in the eye unless they are being aggressive, mean, or disrespectful, we assume that's the way all people operate. If friendly people shake our hand with a weak grip, but people who want to exert their power over us squeeze it tightly, we notice, at least unconsciously.

Many of our school's impoverished parents, especially those who came from a Latino background, learned exactly those lessons. When they came to our school, they were, as anthropologist Kalervo Oberg (1960) said, like "fish out of water" (p. 177). When we shook their hands heartily to express confidence, sincerity, and happiness that they had come, they felt as if we were domineering and aggressive. When we looked them straight in the eye instead of only glancing and then lowering our gaze, they read the same message. When we went straight to talking about their children's grades and did not stop first to ask them about how things were with them, what the names of their other children were, and what their children liked to do, they saw us as unconcerned with them, people concerned about business only.

We taught our staff these cultural differences. We wanted the parents to feel comfortable. If they felt comfortable, they could start to trust us, and with that trust, we could build a good working relationship. Some thought it was the parents' responsibility to adapt to the dominant culture. Who would blink first in a war between ways of being? Our impoverished parents would adapt in time, especially if we acted as a cultural bridge. But we did not have time to wait for them to figure it all out without our help. Their children's futures hung in the balance.

We blinked, and the rewards were immense. Our teachers didn't find it particularly hard to shake hands with a loose grip; say, "Hola," or "Bienvenidos"; and ask what the other children liked to do after school. Simply put, if we value people, we will make them feel at ease when they come to visit us, and that means we need to know what makes them feel uncomfortable and what makes them feel warm and welcomed.

Explanation of How the System Worked

As shown on our agenda, we took time to explain things that we might have assumed everyone knew. Our counselor put together a paper (see fig. 3.7, page 54) that explained how our school was organized. We used the paper as a prompt to explain how credits were earned and what it took to graduate. We showed parents how to read a transcript and how grades were determined. We even clearly explained why having good attendance at school was important and what the consequences of poor attendance were. True, these were things that we could explain at a parent-teacher association (PTA) meeting or hand out at an open house. But our parents weren't attending PTA meetings or coming to our open houses. Besides, we wanted them to really understand and remember this information. Having a conversation about how the system worked while looking at their child's grades, credits, and attendance records made it relevant.

After our new system was in place, we only had to go over this information with the freshman class and any new students who arrived. As younger brothers and sisters grew old enough to enroll in the high school, their parents already knew the score from learning it with their older children. The parents were fully on board, and we could implement the new system without any delays.

Academic Data

Most high school conferences addressed progress reports, attendance records, and transcripts with parents, but we had to go beyond that. Ours was a failing school, with the majority of students performing below grade level in reading, writing, and math. These underlying deficits in basic skills were a powerful current flowing beneath the surface that affected our students' ability to keep up with rigorous learning. If students did not have the necessary skill sets, they would be handicapped when it came to higher education and careers. If they could not pass the Washington Assessment of Student Learning (WASL) exam, they would not graduate. Having honest conversations with our parents and students, not only about their grades, but also about their skills, was crucial.

From the time we began our new system, we used a personalized education plan, or PEP (see fig. 3.8 on pages 55–57), to guide how we talked about where students were academically. We divided this plan into four sections: personal identifying information, data about skill sets, lists of what each party could do about skills deficits, and commitment to action/accountability.

Granger High School
General Information

Key Terms

- SCHOOL YEAR—180 days. The school year is divided into two semesters (90 school days) and four quarters (45 school days).
- REPORT CARDS—A record of students' level of achievement. Report cards are given out at the end of each quarter and semester. Grades earned at a passing level at the end of the semester receive credit.
- CREDIT—A unit that a student is awarded for earning a passing grade (A–D grades). A half credit (0.5) is awarded at the end of each semester. This happens twice yearly.
- TRANSCRIPT—A record of students' semester grades and credits that is updated at the end of each semester. At the end of the senior year, it shows all semester grades since ninth grade.
- GRADE POINT AVERAGE—A calculation of points that students are awarded for every passing grade. Points are as follows:

  A = 4.0, A- = 3.7, B+ = 3.3, B = 3.0, B- = 2.7, C+ = 2.3, C = 2.0, C- = 1.7, D+ = 1.3, D = 1.0, F = 0
- GRADUATION REQUIREMENTS—The classes and other necessary things that students must do to earn a Granger High School diploma.
- CERTIFICATE OF ACADEMIC ACHIEVEMENT—A certificate that is awarded to students who achieve mastery on all parts of the Washington Assessment of Student Learning (WASL) test, which is required to graduate.
- FOUR Ps—Plan, pathway, portfolio, and project.

Graduation Requirements

- ❏ English: 4 credits
- ❏ Mathematics: 3* credits
- ❏ Science: 2* credits
- ❏ Social Studies: 3 credits
  - World History (ninth grade)
  - U.S. History (tenth grade)
  - Contemporary World Problems (twelfth grade)

- ❏ Physical Education: 2 credits
- ❏ Health 9: 0.5 credit
- ❏ Vocational Educational: 3.5 credits
- ❏ Computer Applications: 0.5 credit
- ❏ Electives: 9* credits

Total: 27.5 credits

- ❏ Certificate of Academic Achievement

- ❏ Four Ps

*College-bound students need an extra year of advanced math and science and two years (credits) of a foreign language (as part of their electives).

Figure 3.7: Granger High School general information.

Personalized Education Plan

The purpose of this plan is to provide information and strategies for educators, caregivers, and students to work together to help the student be a successful learner.

School Year: _____

Student's Name: _____ Birth Date: _____

Grade Level: _____ Advisor: _____

Parent/Guardian Name: _____ Telephone: _____

Date of Parental Notification: 1. _____ 2. _____
3. _____

Academic Information

Reading Level: _____ Math Level: _____

MAP Scores: Reading: _____ Language: _____
Math: _____

WASL Scores (7th grade): Reading (400 passing): _____
Writing (12 passing): _____ Math (400 passing): _____
Science (400 passing): _____ (Circle tests that were passed.)

WASL Scores (10th grade): Reading (400 passing): _____
Writing (12 passing): _____ Math (400 passing): _____
Science (400 passing): _____ (Circle tests that were passed.)

Attendance: Excellent Good Fair Poor (circle one)

If you marked Fair or Poor, please write a short explanation: _____

Career Interest: _____

COOPERATIVE FAMILY/SCHOOL INTERVENTION PLAN

Classroom/School Interventions:

Teacher Signature:

Family Interventions:

Caregiver Signature:

Continued →

Student Responsibilities:

Student Signature:

Revised Interventions:

Teacher Initials: Caregiver Initials: Student Initials: Date:

Personalized Education Plan: Possible Interventions

Classroom/School Interventions

- Sustained silent reading
- Classrooms are Essential Academic Learning Requirement relevant*
- Advisory
- Grade check
- Reading in content area
- Problems of the period
- Orchard math
- Math in other classes
- Before-school/after-school study session
- Daily entry task
- Scrabble/chess/cribbage
- Rewire Reading
- Conferences
- Grade checks

Family Interventions

- Set aside one half-hour reading time
- Clarify your academic expectations for your child
- Take away privileges
- Add back privileges as student makes progress
- Provide rewards
- Monitor homework
- Sit with student when working on homework
- Create distraction-free workspace
- Allow sibling assistance on homework
- Provide household quiet time
- Set early bedtime

*Essential Academic Learning Requirements are the standards that students in Washington State must meet.

Student Responsibilities

- Read for one half-hour nightly
- Attend before-school/after-school study session
- Ask questions in class
- Do the work in class
- Retake quizzes/tests
- Turn in assignments
- Increase quality of work
- Choose a positive attitude

- Believe in yourself—you can do it!
- Get enough sleep
- Organize your time
- Use your agenda to write down assignments
- Use your agenda to write down due dates
- Bring back progress reports

Figure 3.8: Our PEP form.

Take reading as a subject example of how we would talk with parents and students. We had a lot of data points that we could share with parents about how well students were doing in reading. The students' reading levels were taken from the Gates-MacGinitie test and showed the grade level at which they were reading. The MAP scores came from a computerized assessment that was even more descriptive of what students could and could not do. And the WASL exams gave us information on how the students did as seventh graders and again as sophomores. We could explain what all of this data meant in our conversations with the parents. More important, we could explain why the results mattered so much, how their child had gotten behind, and what they could do about it. Being able to explain all this to the parents meant that we first had to explain it to our teachers. So we took time in our professional development sessions to do so.

What made our conversations unique was that they didn't stop with talk. After we—parents, students, and teachers—were clear about what the problems were, we jointly created an action plan to solve the problem. We did this in the section titled "Cooperative Family/School Intervention Plan" (see fig. 3.8, page 55). This action plan started with the school: what would the school do to intervene in this student's reading problem? The next section of the PEP listed a menu of possible interventions that the school could use, which gave us a chance to explain the programs we already had in place.

When we first began doing our conferences, reading was such a concern that we had begun doing sustained silent reading (SSR) with all students in our advisory classes, four days a week. As we told the parents about what we were doing, we wrote "SSR" in the box for Classroom/School Interventions. We then explained to the parents that SSR was one of the most important things that students could do to improve their reading skills. We provided a library full of books that were labeled with reading levels. Students only had to choose a book at the appropriate level and find a topic they were interested in, and then bring it to advisory consistently and read. If the students were enrolled in a class using Rewire Reading, we would also explain that program, and we asked the students to tell us what content-area reading strategies their teachers had been giving them to use. The advisor would write each of these activities in the Classroom/School Intervention box.

But we didn't stop there. While talking about SSR, the advisor would ask the student how he or she felt about his or her reading. What was the student reading in SSR, and did he or she like it? Did he or she find it easy, or was it hard to concentrate? Because SSR happened in advisory, the advisor could give his or her feedback: "You know, I notice I really have to remind you often to stop talking during SSR and start reading. What do you think the problem is?"

Such a question became a catalyst to explore the obstacle and create customized solutions. If a student reported that too many people in the classroom were talking and being distractive, the teacher could commit—in writing—to finding a way to keep the class quieter. If the student was sitting too near distracting friends, the teacher could agree to change the seating chart, again writing down this action in the Classroom/School Interventions box. If the student said that reading was boring, the teacher could write, "Personal appointment during advisory with the librarian to find good books/magazines," connecting the student with a valuable resource who could better help the student. Just as likely, the student might agree to write in the Student Responsibilities box, "Make a list of magazines and books I would like after talking to librarian and friends," or "Go to the grocery store and look through all the magazines to find one that I might like." The three-party team might even come up with the idea to "make a pros and cons chart titled 'Why It's Important to Read' during advisory and share it with parents and teacher," and the student would write that down as a responsibility in finding a solution to his or her obstacle.

Parents would commit to making sure their children read thirty minutes or more each night, and students would commit to doing it. The three parties might discuss how likely it was that the student would comply; this was radically new behavior, after all, and new behaviors can be difficult to maintain. The team would explore the idea of taking away privileges if the student did not do the reading and what, specifically, those privileges might be. The parents might agree to have thirty minutes of no TV quiet time for the whole family each night. Or the student might even write down, "I won't say that reading sucks anymore. I'll have a better attitude."

These conferences were powerful, and they worked. Of course, the system was built for human beings, and human beings have been known to foul up almost any system. For this reason, our PEP form also had a box for Revised Interventions. If what we first planned together was not working, we needed to try again. I believe in the power of little tweaks. For example, the cars on the NASCAR circuit are, by rule, pretty much all the same. The difference between the consistent winners and the others is in the cumulative effects of all the little tweaks the mechanics make to the cars and the small changes in techniques and tactics that the drivers make as they hone their craft.

Of course, we also had interventions for improving math skills and writing skills (see chapter 6), but the process was the same as with reading. We identified the skill, discussed where students were currently, and then looked at options for how to improve. We figured out a plan, and everyone was clear about the plan and knew what part he or she would play to make sure the work was getting done to keep everything on track.

Results of Our New System

The powerful potential of the new system was easy to anticipate. But what were the results when we actually implemented the system in the real world? See figure 3.9.

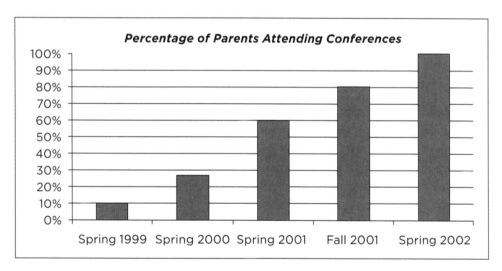

Percentage of Parents Attending Conferences

Figure 3.9: The improvement in our parent engagement.

Remember that in the spring of 2000, we had switched to evening conferences and had completed our home visitations. The results were disappointing: 27 percent of parents attended the conferences. It took us until the spring of 2001 to put the pieces in place for our new communication system, but when we implemented it, we immediately jumped to roughly a 60 percent participation level—a huge improvement to be sure, but not yet where we wanted to be. Still, I predicted that we were on the right path. You cannot break down a culture of disengagement in one year. I thought the students and parents who were afraid of the new system needed time to talk to people who had actually attended conferences. When parents heard from their family, friends, and neighbors that these new conferences were a good thing, they would decide to come the next time.

My prediction proved true. The next fall, we hit about 80 percent attendance without making any significant changes to the system and without making a greater effort to persuade the parents to come. But as I analyzed which parents did not attend conferences in the fall of 2001—the missing 20 percent—and looked at the academic records of their kids, I realized they all had an uncanny resemblance to the family who had inspired our new system a year and a half earlier: Mrs. Cordoba and son.

Getting to 100 Percent

After the conference week ended, I encouraged staff to get all of their missing parents to come in. Teachers made phone calls to try to reschedule conferences; some staff showed up unannounced in the evening at the homes of wayward parents. Stories of those successful forays were retold in the staff room, helping teachers envision new possibilities. Some teachers made use of our home visitor by asking her to make contact with a family. Bit by bit, we chipped away at our reluctant students and families. Still, all these efforts were not enough. The Mrs. Cordobas of our world were still out there.

Prior to the spring conferences of 2002, someone pointed out that if we were going to register students for their next-semester classes at our conferences, why not just require all parents to show up or the student could not register? I knew that if an angry parent challenged me, I probably could not win, but I decided it was worth a calculated risk. How many parents would be unashamed to stand up and declare that they were not willing to meet for thirty minutes, at a time and place convenient for them, in order to plan a schedule that met their child's educational needs? So we announced to our students that they would have to attend conferences with their parents or they would not be able to register, and we gave them a letter stating the same information to carry home to their parents. I did not tell a single person on my staff that this requirement was all a bluff. As far as everyone knew, that was the rule, and we were sticking to it. My bluff would be found out only if someone called me on it.

No one did. At the end of our spring 2002 conferences, some teachers had 100 percent attendance, but others did not. I spoke to each teacher personally and offered new ideas for how to approach the remaining families. Sometimes the family had another child currently enrolled, and we could get two advisors to team up on setting up a joint conference. At our faculty meetings, I asked the whole staff if anyone had any information on particular families or knew who they hung out with or if they ever saw them around the community where we could make contact with them. I asked our social service specialists—drug and alcohol, parent outreach, police, home visitor—and our special education teacher whether they had ever communicated with the family and whether they could give us insights or assistance in making the connections. For some of our most troubled families and students, we called meetings, during which our social services team, special education teacher, counselor, and I met with the student and his or her family to create plans that were custom designed for these students. Their level of need was greater than average, so we met them with a greater-than-average level of expert support.

It was almost the last week of school when the one remaining parent who had not yet been in for a conference came in for his appointment, and we made history. One hundred percent of our high school students' parents had come in to sit at a table and talk about the very important building blocks of their children's futures. One hundred percent of our students had sat down with a concerned educator and taken the time to get real about where each stood, where each wanted to go, and what they—not just students, but parents and educators as well—were going to do about it.

We celebrated with a special assembly and root beer floats in the cafeteria. Then I quieted the students down and explained how remarkable it was that all of their parents had come in, because I didn't think it had ever been done before. I held up two envelopes and opened them, revealing that inside each was a crisp $50 bill. I told them that if anyone could find a public, not private, high school in the state of Washington that was open to all students (in other words, did not selectively admit students like a charter school) that had 100 percent of its parents attend conferences, then the student who found it would receive a $50 bill. The contents of the second envelope awaited anyone who found such a high school anywhere in the nation. Those two $50 bills remained unclaimed. It was truly a remarkable achievement, but that spring was just the start.

Once we hit 100 percent attendance, we had created a new expectation. Yes, the teachers still had to reach out to reluctant parents, but we hit 100 percent again the next fall. Then we did it again in the spring of 2003. I really knew the culture had changed when a student from another district transferred to our school and was placed in my advisory. As we approached another conference week, we talked in advisory about what we would be doing. The new student's hand went up. "What if I don't want to come to a conference, or what if my parents won't come?" he asked. There was a collective "WHAT?" in the room, and several voices chimed in almost simultaneously saying, "Everyone comes to conferences at our school." In a few short years, our students had gone from actively keeping their parents out of the loop when it came to their school lives to being proud of just how unique they were—and justifiably so.

By the time I left Granger High School in June 2008, we had achieved 100 percent attendance at parent conferences thirteen straight times. We had 100 percent for six years in a row.

Results Greater Than the Numbers

More impressive than the 100 percent participation we achieved as a result of our communication system were the changes we saw in our parents, teachers, and—most important—our students.

Parents

As a result of our insisting that parents meet with us and because our teachers made little adjustments that would make parents feel more comfortable, parents came to school and then continued to come back. I cannot tell you the number of parents who took me aside and thanked me for making them feel welcome.

We supported parents with language translation by using the same bilingual para-educators who worked with their children during the day. (This was one of our few extra expenses. Paraeducators were not usually paid to work during conference time, so I pulled money from special programs, such as Title I, to pay for their time. Because these programs all had parent engagement components, this shift was no barrier.) Often, students themselves served as translators, but we let our teachers know that if the parents were smiling and nodding as a student went over his or her grades, but the grades were not good, we had paraeducators available to serve as both translators and truth serum. After we had one meeting with a family and the parents understood the routine, they would sometimes bring along an older child, other relative, or neighbor to help translate for them, so language barriers rapidly faded as an issue.

The parents felt empowered because they got clear direction on what their students needed to do, and they knew they had the right, and responsibility, to ask their kids to do it.

Parents Knew Who to Call to Get Answers

Where once the school was a strange and scary institution in our parents' minds, now the school had a face—it might be the face of Mr. Garza or of Miss Vickers. The advisor became the parents' liaison to the school. In the past, if parents talked to their child at home about why he or she had a poor grade on a progress report and the student blamed the teacher, the matter usually stopped there. Parents who were not engaged with the school were not about to leap cultural and language barriers to talk to a teacher they did not know.

Under our new system, parents had a friend in the business, so to speak. The advisor could answer their questions or even talk with the teacher in question to get his or her perspective. Parents were never stuck with only one side of the story. They knew they had an advocate who would help them communicate with other teachers, even if that meant the advisor went with them to sit in on a meeting with another teacher.

Parents Felt Supported and Empowered

Our conferences became the semiannual event when parents and teens talked seriously and in detail about the student's educational progress and his or her plans for the future. At a time when most families' teens don't even want to talk with their parents about how their day was, we set up a mechanism for parents to talk to their children about important things. Because we set up the structure, all they had to do was show up.

A teacher empowers a parent when he or she asks, "Are there privileges you could take away if your child doesn't do what he promises?" It is helpful to have an adult from outside the family say to the child just what the parent has been saying all along: "Sometimes, you have to do things in life that you don't feel like doing, but look into the future and see why this is important." It is also helpful when the student starts lashing out against the parent to have a teacher there to defuse the situation: "I understand why you feel angry right now, and it's natural, but let's take a deep breath. It's not your mom you should be mad at. She wants to help you. Let's look at the problem."

The teachers and parents didn't team up against the student. The teacher mediated the power struggles that parents and teens go through while battling over subpar performance in school. The teacher pointed the way back to the issue and away from blame in a shoulder-to-shoulder maneuver and, thus, was usually able to bring emotions back in check. If we had an extravolatile family, we brought in a counselor or other support personnel to help mediate.

We truly created a system that empowered and supported parents in their attempts to encourage educational achievement. Through our discussions, these parents learned to track their kids and follow through better than they could have without our help.

The system was not perfect in all cases, however, nor was it a panacea. There is a world of discouragement and brokenness out there. The alcoholic parents remained alcoholics. The same parents who were hard to get in for conferences one year were usually hard to get in the next year. But the rising tide of our conferences lifted the boats of all families. Families on the margin moved away from the edge of dysfunctional communication until they were no longer marginal, giving us more energy to focus on the truly dire cases. The truly dire cases showed improvement because we had all parties at the table and applied the power of all our resources to them.

Teachers

Our conferences brought about big changes for our teachers as well. Change is not just a nice bonus; it is an essential feature in improving any system. Although our teachers were smart and well intentioned, they had unwittingly played a part in the old, failed system.

Teachers Climbed Out of Their Silos

Teachers tended to work in isolation. They knew a lot about their subjects but not always how many science credits were required for graduation or what services were available for assisting students who struggled with writing. Our system helped to educate teachers about such areas as much as it did the parents. Teachers went from not knowing what it took to graduate to knowing how to help students think about their career goals and work through the decisions about what classes to take. No longer were they just teaching a subject such as health or history. Now teachers were teaching students and participating in the molding of their students' lives and futures.

Teachers Took Ownership of Their Advisees

When the teachers knew they were responsible for 150 students, and the majority of those students were struggling, they felt understandably overwhelmed. Becoming responsible for only twenty students lightened their burden. As teachers built relationships with their twenty students, fewer students got lost in the system. We did not turn all of them around immediately, but we did a better job of supporting students and parents. When progress reports came out, advisors were the first to know how their students were doing and had the opportunity to talk to their students during advisory time.

Teachers Became More Proactive in Contacting Parents

There is no doubt in my mind that many teachers were uncomfortable contacting parents, because of their past experiences of encountering aggressive parents or parents who did not seem to care. The conference-time conversations minimized that discomfort. If students were struggling to stick to academic action plans, our advisors were much more likely to call parents than in the past. Sometimes, they called at the request of another teacher, in whose class the student was doing poorly. Sometimes teachers called because they noticed poor performance on the progress report and they had promised, as part of the action plan, that they would let the parents know if their student was deviating from that plan.

Although some individual teachers continued to call parents about their students' progress in their class, more and more, our advisors played a role. Sometimes, they became facilitators between families of their advisees and another teacher when a serious issue needed to be worked out. This mediation resulted in less adversarial stances by some of our parents. After all, it is harder to bluster against someone who shows you kindness and understanding than it is against a faceless representative of the educational establishment. The rapport that advisors established with parents could then be lent to other teachers with whom the advisor teamed up to solve students' obstacles.

Teachers Changed Their Attitudes

In the past, when teachers saw that our parents were disengaged from their children's education, it was easy to blame the parents. When teachers heard rumors about an alcoholic parent or an absent parent, they felt helpless. When teachers learned the statistics of the poor academic prognosis for impoverished and minority students, that knowledge made their jobs seem hopeless. No one who is stuck in blaming and helplessness and hopelessness can start a revolution.

We started our revolution by giving teachers a structure to make their jobs more manageable, knowledge so they could answer questions about how to overcome obstacles that were blocking student achievement, and resources to refer to when they didn't know the answers. Our teachers were less likely to blame parents and more likely to look for ways to get them involved. Although they could not create utopias, our teachers knew they had the capacity to really make a difference for even our neediest families, and many did just that. As Henry Ford said, "Whether you think you can or you think you can't, you're right." Our teachers started to think they could, and so they did.

Students

Hiding the progress reports was no longer enough after parents made a personal connection to an adult at school. What students had previously done in secret was now being broadcast from the rooftops. All the talk about the importance of getting a good education turned into something much more real and unavoidable. In our conferences, we were talking about life-changing stuff with our students: Which of the three roads of life are you on? (See chapter 7.) How can we help you to change course, and just as important, what are you going to do about it?

Student-Led Conferences Led to Ownership of Results

The conferences became student-led meetings, with the teacher acting as an interpreter of the information and a facilitator of the process. The students explained what and how they were doing in classes, what they were doing to learn more about the careers that interested them, and what they were doing to improve their reading, writing, and math skills. Having students lead the conferences was a small but important shift that reflected the reality of the students' situation: they were in charge of their education; what they did or did not do meant everything.

Students Felt Supported

Students also learned that they were not alone. The conferences were not opportunities for student bashing; they were a chance to celebrate achievements and, at the same time, to analyze obstacles to success in order to figure out how to overcome them. Although the truth was hard for some students, an honest look allowed us to ask questions about what they wanted from their futures and determine if they were on the right path to get it. If not, we offered them additional learning opportunities, ways to get back on track. We made agreements about what each party would do to help students achieve their goals. The action plans may not have been comfortable, and the students may not have liked the agreements, but all our students knew that they were not alone. Even if we could never get their parents fully on board, the students still had their advisors, which was more than many of them had ever had before.

The Real Reason Behind Our Success

Our success was not based on our changing to student-led conferences, nor was it based on the fact that we required our parents to attend. Changing the structure of a program alone will not get the job done. Checking off a list of strategies will not ensure amazing results.

The whole point in communicating with students and their parents is truly caring about both, and caring enough that we offer to guide them through this sometimes difficult, sometimes joyous process of life that we call education. Isn't caring the entire reason we went into education in the first place? Didn't we all dream of having a tremendous impact on the lives of those we taught? If the dream has dulled over the years, if you have become somewhat less idealistic and a little more jaded, I want to encourage you to recapture your first passion. Do not shrink back from pursuing the dream anew. Do not set limits on how many kids you can really reach. I can assure you that the teachers on my staff transformed lives.

Please read the next chapter about our mentorship program at Granger with your full attention. Our efforts would have been much less effective without the warm, caring heart of mentorship beating inside the cold, skeletal structure of our program. Don't use your intellectual brilliance to build the educational equivalent of Dr. Frankenstein's monster; give your creation a heart.

Chapter 4

MENTORSHIP

This chapter shows how we changed our system and our practices to make mentorship a key focus. I truly believe that we would not have had the impact we had in turning Granger High School from a school with an 80–90 percent failure rate into one with an 80–90 percent success rate without the mentorship aspects of our advisory program.

Why Advisories?

Advisories are not new. They came into widespread use in the 1970s as a reaction to the student unrest of the '60s and '70s but faded away in the 1980s. The idea of advisories began to shift again, however, with the push for standards-based education when the emphasis on increased rigor for all students demanded a closer look at the supports necessary to accomplish the goal. Advisories were now being promoted as a way to personalize education by creating a place where relevance (why we study this stuff) and relationship (meaningful connections to school personnel) could be brought into the picture.

The Center for Secondary School Redesign (CSSR) says that "when done well, advisories build relationships between students and strengthen bonds with teachers, changing the way students feel about school and improving the educational experience for the entire school community" (CSSR, n.d.). The key phrase is "when done well." As the title of this chapter suggests, it's my belief that a well-implemented advisory will involve mentorship.

What do advisors do? They advise; they tell people what to do or what they would do if they were in another's shoes. Our advisors offered advice, but I encouraged them to go beyond that and become mentors. What do mentors do? A mentor is someone who has experience in life and who not only advises, but also serves as an example of how to negotiate the journey of life. A poem that John Wooden often quoted, one he learned as a young teacher, captures it:

> No written word, no spoken plea,
> Can teach our youth what they should be.
> Nor all the books on all the shelves.
> It's what the teachers are themselves.
> —Anonymous

The first "mentor" was a character in Homer's great tale *The Odyssey*. Mentor—that was his actual name—was put in charge of Odysseus's household when he went off to the Trojan War. Mentor was to watch over Odysseus's young son, overseeing his care while the warrior was away, guiding him and teaching him all that he needed to know. I see the power of mentorship in our schools in that original story of Mentor. Parents entrust us with the care of their children while they go off to face the daily battle of making a living. While they are away, we are to care for their offspring and help them to develop and grow by using all of our wisdom to prepare them for all that lies ahead. In order to work effectively with our students, I believe we need to do more than just talk to them and try to fill their heads with knowledge.

I encouraged the teachers to take care of their advisory students as if the students were their own kids. In my mind, that meant the following three things:

1. Keep track of their attendance.
2. Keep track of their grades and skill sets.
3. Help them figure out what they want to do with their lives.

Teachers did these three things and then coached their students to persevere. I call this method the "three-plus-one model of mentorship": three things to track plus coaching the mentees to keep working until they reached their goals. This three-plus-one model is what I believe led to 100 percent of the students in my advisory graduating on time (in four years). Mentorship works.

The Math of Mentorship

A typical high school teacher with five or six classes, each containing thirty students, has a student load of 150–180, meaning the student-to-teacher ratio is 150:1 or 180:1. The typical student-to-counselor ratio is approximately 400:1, or even 600:1 for some schools. Is it any wonder that kids sometimes get lost in the system?

If being responsible for a high number of students were really a good thing, you would expect to see such numbers where they matter most: on sports teams. That last statement was only half in jest, because most communities take various sports programs very seriously. Could a sports team get away with having one coach for every 180–400 athletes? Most communities would not stand for it. They know that it takes more hands-on training from coaches than that to prepare athletes for competition, so our sports teams have athlete-to-coach ratios more in line with 30:1, 20:1, or even 15:1.

If we feel it is important to provide low athlete-to-coach ratios, why do we not do the same thing with teachers? At Granger, we could not provide a 20:1 ratio in all of our classes because we did not have the budget. But what we could do was create a mentorship program so that every student would be cared for in a class in which the student-to-teacher ratio did not exceed 20:1.

But reducing the student-to-teacher ratio to 20:1 was only the start. In our failing school, graduation rates indicated that at least one-third of the students were at risk of failure. We could never hire enough counselors to help so great a number. The numbers meant that each of our teachers typically had fifty to sixty students on their rosters who were at risk of not graduating or, just as bad, of graduating with inadequate skills to be lifelong learners. That is an overwhelming number for just about any teacher. But through the mentorship program, each advisor would have no more than five to seven at-risk students in his or her mentorship class.

Development of Our Mentorship Program

In the spring of 1999, the end of my first year at Granger, we embarked on a school-improvement planning process through which our team identified reading skills as our number-one need for improvement. We wanted our students to develop a love of reading so that they would read for pleasure and thus practice, practice, practice. The previous principal had instituted a fifteen-minute SSR block in the schedule, but the planning team wanted to expand it to thirty minutes to create more practice time. I saw this as the perfect opportunity to set up an advisory program at the same time. I talked to the team about the importance of building relationships of trust with our students and suggested that we set up our reading practice in an advisory class, limited to eighteen to twenty students per teacher. The initial focus would be on SSR, but I knew we could shift the focus to mentorship as time went on.

We rearranged our schedule, starting the next fall (August 2000), by getting rid of a fifteen-minute daily block of time that was devoted to watching Channel 1, the satellite news program, and adding that time to the fifteen-minute daily SSR program that was already in place. We moved this thirty-minute block of time to the end of the day. We also added a ninety-minute staff-development period on Wednesdays to the four-period A/B alternating block schedule that the school had implemented shortly before I arrived. (On Monday, classes 1A, 2A, and 4A met for ninety minutes; on Tuesday, classes 1B, 2B, and 4B met; and the classes alternated every other day. The schedule also included a "skinny class" that met every day during third period for fifty minutes.)

Just-in-Time Staff Development

Our once-weekly staff development was the school equivalent of the just-in-time manufacturing process that Toyota used to revolutionize the quality of automobiles. Instead of mass-producing and stockpiling parts, Toyota produced parts in smaller batches. The components were ready just as they were needed in the assembly process. By making this change, Toyota was able to incorporate what it had learned about the components: their strengths and weaknesses and how they fit into the overall systems of the vehicle. Toyota then had the time to make critical tweaks to how the components were manufactured, improving the parts according to continuously updated information.

In the same way, we used just-in-time weekly staff development to look at the performances of students and the system in which they were working. Instead of mass-producing educational strategies, our teachers were better able to come up with innovative tweaks that would help students be more successful. By not having to deal with problems that might not come up for several months, our teachers were able to focus on what was most pressing, in the present.

During the first year of our advisories (2000–2001), our hands were full during our staff-development times because of all the changes we were trying to accomplish in the first year of our school-improvement process. To focus on the mentorship aspect of our schedule would have been a mistake. We simply did not have enough mental space left to focus on mentorship properly, and it would have gotten lost had we tried to tackle it at that time.

Instead, we just did SSR and let discussions of mentorship stay at a surface level most of that first year. It wasn't until the second semester, as we began to talk about implementing our three-way communication system with the parent conferences, that we began to focus more on the idea of mentorship. At first, we tied our staff development directly to what we wanted to accomplish with our conferences: to talk to all parents about where their children were now and where they wanted to go, and to enlist the parents' support in helping their children take responsibility for doing what it took to be successful. Our school counselor and I presented ideas, and the staff gave us feedback about what they thought needed to happen. In this way, we created the forms and format for our conferences.

Later, the counselor explained the graduation requirements and taught teachers how to help their students create a course schedule, allowing the teachers to work with actual student data so they gained confidence. Teachers were then able to go into their advisory classes and help their advisees put together their schedules and answer questions.

Nothing about this method was magic. It was simply just-in-time staff development, guided by the needs of the moment and taught in the most practical way possible. What the teachers needed, we worked on learning together. What we learned, we immediately implemented.

To get two hours of continuous staff-development time every week, I made a deal with my staff. If they would stay an extra thirty minutes each week beyond our ninety-minute scheduled session, I would let them leave on Fridays as soon as the buses cleared our parking lots instead of making them wait until the contracted thirty minutes after the final bell. I had to get a waiver with the teachers' union to make this offer official, but I found this thirty minutes to be a much more productive use of time on Wednesdays than on Fridays, and it bought me a great deal of goodwill. (I did have one teacher who refused to stay the extra time on Wednesdays, and that was his right as a professional.)

Our Purpose

In my opinion, the most helpful factor for guiding schools in conducting advisories right is found in the title of one of CSSR's training manuals: *Advisories With a Purpose*. The purpose for advisories in your school does not have to be exactly the same as that of another school, and it probably should not be if you want to address your unique institutional, community, and cultural needs. However, clarifying what that purpose is will set the stage for you to achieve your outcomes with much more uniformity and much less frustration and defensive behaviors on the part of your staff.

In the spirit of building a plane while flying it, we lifted off with a clearly defined purpose: reading. Once under way we added the pieces necessary to get to our true purposes: motivation and mentorship. Eventually, we defined five purposes as a school, which we cobbled together from language we saw used by other schools with advisories:

1. Every student will be well known, both personally and academically, by at least one staff member.

2. Every student will be pushed to increase his or her reading level and math level.

3. Every student will be challenged to meet rigorous academic standards in an appropriate educational program.

4. Every student will be provided with opportunities to experience the benefits of community membership and to develop and practice leadership skills.

5. Every student will be prepared for whatever he or she chooses to do after graduation, with a strong transcript, a career pathway, a plan, and a portfolio.

Selecting Advisors

If you taught full time in our school, you were an advisor. If you taught part time, you might be an advisor or share an advisory with another teacher, depending on when you were scheduled to be in the building. During our first year of advisories, I shared an advisory with our school counselor. After a few years' hiatus, I took an advisory on by myself and took a group of freshmen through their four years at Granger High School. I think my being an advisor made the students take the advisories more seriously. After all, if even the principal is leading an advisory, it must be important stuff.

There are many examples available of large high schools and middle schools that are able to adequately staff effective advisory programs. Size really doesn't matter; everyone can get to a low student-to-advisor ratio if they choose. In fact, I asked one of my staff members to do some research on the State of Washington, and we found that by taking the total number of students and dividing it by the number of teachers and building administrators, the average student-to-adult ratio was 20:1.

Selecting Students

Our advisories were broken up by grade level: freshmen with freshmen, and so on. We used the following criteria to balance our advisories:

- **Reading skill**. We wanted a heterogeneous mix, so we scattered good readers among average and poor readers. After we had all our students' reading scores in a spreadsheet, it was easy enough to do this by re-sorting the students from highest to lowest to get a rank order. Then we did the following:

  - We placed the number-one ranked reader in advisory 1, the number-two reader in advisory 2, and so on. For example, if there were four freshmen advisories, we placed students 1 through 4 each in a separate advisory.

  - Then we placed the number-five ranked reader in advisory 4; the number-six reader in advisory 3, the number-seven reader in advisory 2, and the number-eight reader in advisory 1.

  - We repeated this process until we reached the bottom of the rank-order list.

- **Gender**. After we completed the initial list based on reading scores, we further refined it based on gender. If there was a significant imbalance of boys to girls in an advisory, we looked at how to swap students with similar reading levels.

- **At-risk classification**. We tried to balance the students who were most at risk so that no advisor had more than five to seven such students. If we overloaded a particular advisor, we carefully swapped students to balance the load. Usually, the reading level did this automatically, but it was important to double-check.

- **Advisor recommendation**. Finally, if an advisor knew a student and recognized some impediment to building rapport (personality conflicts, previously demonstrated bad relationships with the parents, or such), then the advisor could request a trade. Or, if the advisor had already established rapport with a student or knew that a student possessed talents or interests that lined up particularly well with the advisor, he or she could trade with another advisor for that student.

The use of reading skills as our first sorting criteria helped us to get a good mix of students with different temperaments and leadership skills, which meant that our stronger students and leaders could help lead their less-developed peers. This mix also meant that we could sustain good discussions on matters important to school success, because of the different perspectives that were present in the room.

We decided that no advisory roster was final. No system could provide the best fit for students 100 percent of the time. If a student did not fit in well with an advisory class, the teacher was free to talk to other advisors about trading students. I asked teachers to use this power judiciously and to talk to the students involved about the process in order to get their buy-in, but the advisors had no limitations on when trades could be made or how often. They were professionals in charge of making decisions about what was best for the kids. I let the staff know that we expected them to do what was right.

Our Mentorship Program Curriculum

Although the three-plus-one model of tracking students and coaching them was a good foundation for our program, it still didn't detail what activities should be done on a day-by-day basis during advisory. Had we left this up to teachers to create, we would have just created another class for them to prep for—which, believe me, we did not want to do and which would have opened the door to wildly divergent effectiveness from advisory to advisory.

We solved this problem by using a combination of programs developed by others and our just-in-time staff development. Before implementing any new program, we taught teachers how it worked during our weekly early release time. Sometimes, outside consultants led these trainings. Sometimes, some of our own staff members learned about the programs and taught the others. Teachers had a chance to discuss how they could adapt a program to better fit our students and purposes. After we implemented the program, we used our just-in-time approach to talk about how things were progressing and to troubleshoot our implementation.

Regardless of the programs and activities selected for use in the advisory program, there is no substitute for devoting adequate time to preimplementation planning for all advisors and ongoing professional learning communities to increase your advisors' skills in leading their students. Failing to plan for advisories really is planning to fail.

Conference Preparation

We required our students to keep a tabbed binder of work that they were doing in their advisory. They kept this binder in the classroom on a shelf or in a cupboard, so we never had to worry about it being lost. The binder contained all the documents the students needed to share with their parents, so when the time came for the semiannual parent conferences, the only thing students had to do was pull out the binder.

We also expected our students to lead their conference with assistance and oversight from the advisor. Student-led conferences had the benefits of making our students think about and evaluate their own progress, own up to their responsibility for their learning, analyze the relevance of what they were learning to their future goals, and learn how to communicate all of this information clearly and honestly to their parents.

Because our students led the conferences, our advisors devoted time to the following activities during advisory in the weeks leading up to the conferences:

- Directing students to organize documents, such as progress reports and transcripts, in their binders

- Going over the agenda for the upcoming conferences with the whole group so students understood what they would have to explain to their parents

- Meeting individually with advisees to look at their binder, discuss their progress, ask what was going on in any classes in which there were low grades and/or missing work, and help students talk about what they would be going over with their parents

Meeting with each advisee gave advisors the chance to be a mentor and an advocate for the student. If students could not explain why they had a bad grade, the mentor would explore the issue with them. If students blamed the teacher for the bad grade or used some other excuse, the mentor walked them through the reasons why blaming others was not productive and encouraged them to take responsibility for the situation, which meant students needed to go to their teachers and talk about the poor grades and what they needed to do to improve. This directive often meant teaching students the skill of how to stand up for themselves while remaining respectful to the person with whom they were in conflict. If the students came back frustrated from such conversations or were already locked in some sort of serious misunderstanding with a teacher, their mentor could become an advocate, standing side-by-side with the student when he or she went to talk to the teacher after school or approaching the other teacher on a colleague-to-colleague basis, if necessary. All of this work served as preparation for productive conferences with the parents, where the truth would be told, problems would be solved, and more solid teamwork would be built to ensure support for all our students to reach their goals.

Progress Reports and Checkups

Because we had so many struggling students, we required progress reports from teachers every two weeks. Most teachers kept their gradebooks updated on the computer, and it took them little time to print out the progress reports. We asked each advisor to monitor closely all his or her students, but especially the most at-risk students. Also, we asked each advisor to make notes on the PEP, which was developed during conferences, about the actions to which students, parents, and the advisor had committed. For example, an advisor might have agreed to check each week on a student's progress in a particular class and either call the parents or send a progress report home to be signed.

Checkups were one- to five-minute miniconferences that the advisors held with their advisees. Checkups usually indicated problems early, before parent intervention was needed. I can honestly say that in my four years as an advisor, I had to make no more than ten phone calls home about progress reports. My process when discussing a poor progress report generally went something like this:

Me: What's going on with algebra? Why an F?

Student: I'm having a hard time understanding how to do the work.

Me: Well, that's what learning is. We don't know something at first, and we struggle with it until we learn it. Are you paying attention in class?

Student: Yes, but I still don't understand how to do the work. I don't always want to ask questions because I don't want to look like I'm dumb.

Me: If you fail the class, what do you think people will think then? But what is worse is that you will be behind with your math credits, which will stop you from graduating and reaching your career goals. It sounds like you're at a point where you're going to need to get some extra help to catch up. When can you come in? We've got our before- and after-school programs, and Mr. Hernandez is in his classroom at lunch.

Student, a bit defensively: OK, I will talk to Mr. Hernandez.

Me: Do you see any other choice?

Student: No. But I really don't want to.

Me: Well, you agreed in our last student conference that if you were failing a class you would come in before or after school for help until you were caught up. Do I have to call your mom to set that up?

Student: No, no. I'll do it.

Me: OK, I'll give you a chance, but you need to tell her that you're going to attend one of the extra sessions every day next week. If you don't show up, I'll have to give her a call. Let's check up on what you've done by next Thursday.

Many teachers think mentorship will entail a lot of extra work, that holding students accountable will mean a lot more phone calls home and dealing with parents. In my experience, fewer calls were needed. And the calls I made were more effective because of the ongoing relationships I had established with the parents and students. Not only was this checkup process easier than the old system of individual teachers making all their own calls, but also it was more effective in raising student achievement.

Careers

In a study by Gail Matthews (n.d.) of Dominican University, 149 adults—entrepreneurs, educators, attorneys, bankers, managers, and so on—worked on achieving self-selected goals for one month. At the end of the month, they were asked to rate their progress and the degree to which they had accomplished their goals. Those participants who wrote down their goals achieved 42 percent more of their goals than those who merely thought about them. Moreover, those who wrote down their goals and shared them with a friend achieved even more: 50 percent greater success than those who only thought about their goals. The individuals who wrote down their goals, shared them with a friend, and wrote weekly progress reports to a friend did the best of all: they achieved 78 percent more of their goals than the participants who just thought about their goals.

We wanted our students to have a written career goal. Our system of mentorship and three-way communication between students, home, and educator team provided the sense of commitment and accountability that Matthews's study so strongly supports. So exploring careers and choosing one or more options became a strong focus of our advisory activities. Further supporting our program were some new state graduation requirements that included "The Four Ps," a plan that included a student's career *pathways*, post–high school *plans*, school *portfolios*, and culminating, senior *projects*. But even without those state requirements, we knew that having tangible goals to work toward would not only make school more bearable, but also it would engage students more deeply. And the more deeply engaged the students were in pursuing their goals through education, the better they would do in life. The stronger the goal, the stronger the effort.

To start our career exploration, we used an online program called Bridges (www .bridges.com), in which our students took aptitude tests, completed personality and values assessments, and were able to look at a vast library of career choices that fit their profiles.

We encouraged students to choose careers that interested them and to explore those options further. The Bridges program showed the pathways necessary to work in a particular field: what kind of postsecondary training was required and what high school courses would prepare students for postsecondary schools. The students then wrote this information in their binder or portfolio.

We also required our students to complete two job shadows in careers of their choice. We used special-programs money to pay our full-time attendance secretary to spend half of her time scheduling job shadows throughout our local communities. The advisors did not have to do anything.

Job shadows were an important part of making the career program relevant. I can still remember the girl who wanted to be a veterinarian until she actually watched a surgery on a dog that had swallowed a ball. The sight of that much blood was all she needed to realize that she wanted to find another career choice. This type of job shadow was the kind of relevant learning experience that helped our students explore who they were and gave them important motivation for their studies.

Projects

As students became seniors, our advisories turned into the perfect forum for them to work on their state-mandated culminating project. These projects required students to demonstrate the ability to think analytically, logically, and creatively to solve problems; to apply what they learned in school to the real world; and then to present the project in front of a panel of adults from the community and school. They could do a research project on a topic of personal interest or a service project to benefit the community. Because our students had been with their advisors for three years, they were in a position to receive strong support from a mentor who knew them and could help guide them through this daunting process.

Test Prep

During our students' junior year, when most of them would take their SAT or ACT tests, we sometimes used advisories for test prep. Because our students' families often could not afford SAT tutors or classes, we purchased software that students could access from their classroom computers.

In addition, during the second half of their sophomore year, we used some advisory periods to focus on preparing students for the upcoming state tests. We worked on the much-maligned, but very successful, tips on how to take tests.

More importantly, we spent time on practice exercises in reading, writing, and math, working in groups to have students evaluate each other's responses and discuss why answers were either right or wrong or, in the case of open-ended response questions that required students to explain their answers, which answers were better and why. This practice helped more students gain the skills to pass the test, and the skills they learned helped them think analytically, read with comprehension, write with fluency and clarity, and solve problems logically. Those are valuable life skills that translate to job success by anyone's measure.

Navigation 101

In the early years of the new millennium, the Franklin Pierce school district in Washington created and refined something it called "Navigation 101" (Office of Superintendent of Public Instruction, n.d.). This program was designed to help students in grades 6–12 do the same kind of career exploration and planning for their future that we were working on. The district was so successful that the state piloted its work with other districts, made refinements, and released it for any school to use as a full curriculum to include the following:

- Implementing curriculum-driven advisories focused on career preparation

- Having students develop portfolios

- Implementing student-led conferences

- Getting students to prepare for and take more rigorous classes

- Using data to analyze the success of the advisory program

We relied heavily on the excellent tools provided by the Navigation 101 program to make sure we were covering what we needed to in order for our students to reach their goals. (Visit www.k12.wa.us/navigation101 for more information about Navigation 101.)

Speakers

When representatives from colleges, vocational schools, or the military wanted to speak to our students, the advisory period was the logical venue. That way, we didn't lose valuable time in our academic classes, and yet we were still able to promote postsecondary options and benefit from the excellent role models and information these institutions sent us. Having these flesh-and-blood representatives stand in front of our students was so much better than handing out a college brochure. These visits made college seem like a reality for students who had never even had a family member graduate from high school.

I was always on the lookout for role models who could inspire our students and show them that what we were saying was true, that hard work and dreams could take them anywhere. One of my brothers, for example, became a relay technician for the Bonneville Power Administration, the company that runs the huge hydroelectric dams that produce power on the Columbia River. He went to vocational school and became an electrician, and after years of good performance and on-the-job learning, he made more money than I made as a high school principal. Having as a guest a Mexican American man who had come from poverty and was able to relate to the students was a real eye-opener for our students. So was the young recruiter from Perry Technical College. He was able to relate to our students and invite them to visit the campus to see all the great things they could become. And when an agent from the Secret Service contacted me to investigate whether I had counterfeited $420,000 (see chapter 7), I even talked him into coming to our school to talk to students about how to become a Secret Service agent.

Of course, we held our whole-school assemblies and class meetings during our advisory period so that they didn't affect teaching time. We used these assemblies to deliver messages on careers and motivation. We did not use advisory as a time to hold club meetings, let students make up tests, or talk to teachers about assignments. Unless there were mitigating circumstances, students and teachers had to take care of that kind of business before or after school, at lunch, or during our ten-minute passing break between first and second periods. The activities in advisory, while flexible, were too important to make a habit of setting them aside.

The School of Life

We found that advisory was the perfect time for us to talk about real-life, or school-of-life, examples of the power of education and how the world really worked. We did this by discussing the stories of people who overcame obstacles like those our students faced through the power of their attitude and their commitment to using education as their way out.

Most kids, in general, don't know a lot about the adult world. They may know the price of a snack wrap at the fast-food restaurant or the cost of the MP3 player they want for their birthday, but many don't have a clue about the cost of cars and houses. For students who grow up in poverty, their understanding about these real-world items is likely to be even more off-base. Many students might talk about "rockin' a Bentley" (luxury automobile) or living in a "phat crib" (comfortable dwelling), but few have done the math to see how much those extravagant items would cost and what kind of income they would need to sustain that kind of lifestyle.

So I brought in the classified ads and had students dream about the kinds of cars they wanted to own. Then I asked students to look up the costs and the monthly payments. We talked about insurance and worked out formulas to see how much a car would cost them over the life of a loan. Very eye-opening stuff. We also looked at the prices for both apartments and houses. We looked at the recommended limits for how much one should spend for housing and then figured out what salary they would have to earn in order to afford different houses.

Some time later, I heard a principal speak at a conference. He had done the same thing with his students but had actually taken them on some field trips as well. First, they went to a used-car dealership and looked at cars. Salespeople showed them the prices of the cars and discussed payment plans and typical insurance and maintenance costs. Next, they went to a Ford dealership and did the same thing. And, finally, they went to a Lexus dealership. Loaded with this real-world information, the students went back to school and did the math on how much they would need to earn to afford the different cars and identified what kind of careers paid that kind of money.

On a second field trip, the principal worked with realtors to first go to a poor neighborhood to look at apartments and houses, then to middle-class and upscale neighborhoods. The realtors not only showed prices, but also talked about how much of a person's income typically went into housing and explained some of the other costs of homeownership, such as taxes, insurance, maintenance, utilities, and down payments and deposits.

Field trips may have had an even greater impact on our students, but I didn't let the fact that our school didn't have the budget hold us back. Advisory allowed us to journey into the school of life without stepping foot off campus.

The School of Hard Knocks

Advisory was also the perfect place for students to deal with tragedies.

Our students arrived at school on a beautiful morning in September 2001 to be greeted by news of something almost incomprehensible: the attack on the World Trade Center. Throughout the day, we certainly held discussions on the topic in our academic classes. Many teachers tuned in and allowed the students to watch the historic proceedings as the day went on. But it was in the end-of-day advisory period where we could really get down to the emotions of the day. The relationships that had been built in each advisory and the freedom for students to talk about their feelings created a forum where students were heard and supported in a dark time.

The next year, one of our brightest and most well-liked students took his own life. That night, we called all our teachers and asked them to come in a few hours early the next morning to meet with a regional crisis intervention team that would brief us on how to handle the situation so it did not escalate, because research shows that suicides are prone to starting a rash of copycat suicides from other students. Our crisis team leaders carefully explained that we had to allow students to express their feelings and ask questions, but we had to be very clear in the message we gave to students: no matter how much we loved this young man, we could not condone his actions.

We started our schedule that day with our students by gathering in advisories and following the discussion plan that the crisis team gave to us. Tears were shared, questions that had no answers were asked, lessons were learned about accepting what we could not know, and anger was expressed. Afterward, we still had a team of counselors available to meet with students in the cafeteria, but we went about our normal day. The students responded very well to this approach. (Will was the boy's advisor, and he felt it best to use a few more advisory periods to allow students to process their thoughts, but most of the other advisories moved forward.) Our message was stated clearly, and there were no copycat attempts.

Advisories cannot prevent the tragedies of life, but when they happen, the relationships built and the time already present in the schedule make advisories an ideal place to teach students how to handle them. For example, when we faced a sudden increase in fights and bullying between a particularly aggressive group of freshmen and sophomore girls, we met in advisories with the freshmen and sophomores to discuss the situation. In this way, we were able to get some emotions out in the open and talk about how to handle these feelings of aggression, but we were also able to use peer pressure from all those who disapproved of these girls' behaviors and clarify how we would handle the issue from the administrative side. The result was that students felt safer because they knew we were watching out for them and because they were watching out for each other.

Fun

Fun does not appear as a goal in too many grant applications for federal funds to improve education. It should. If "all work and no play makes Jack a dull boy," it also makes him dull-witted. I believe fun is important. Fun reduces stress, creates positive emotions that lead to increased engagement, and draws people closer together. Although I believe that learning is its own best reward, teenagers are pretty transparent in their need for fun, and advisories should have a healthy dose.

As chapter 7 explains, we also used advisory for celebrations of student progress, with occasional root beer float parties in the cafeteria when we hit certain benchmarks. One year, after seeing the joy students took in competing for best hallway decorations for Homecoming, we created a holiday door contest, in which each advisory competed to see who could make their doorway the most festive for the December holidays. We also started a contest to see who would be the first advisory to get all their parents in for parent conferences and win bragging rights for the semester.

I was constantly on the lookout to provide little bits of fun with my own advisory, to give my advisees a little spark amid all the work they were doing. Christmas was a big holiday in our area, so I bought stockings for all eighteen of my advisees and hung them in our advisory class. Inside, I put some pencils that we'd had imprinted with our school logo. I also included a 100 Grand candy bar (originally known as the $100,000 bar), which represented the first payment of the $420,000 more they would earn over their lifetime by graduating from high school. In another example, when my students were sophomores, they were all going crazy to get their driver's licenses. To commemorate this event, I put little Hot Wheels cars in their Christmas stockings—surrogates for the fancy full-sized ones they would be able to afford someday if they kept up the hard work. All of their work was going to make these things real one day if they really wanted them.

The Essence of Advisories

As time went on with our advisories, I came to understand that the essential pieces of our advisories were all about three things: "failure is not an option," the Big W, and advisories as families.

The phrase "failure is not an option," which was popularized by the movie *Apollo 13* (Grazer & Howard, 1995), was more of an attitude than a mere advisory precept. In the advisory, the numbers were small enough that it was possible to focus attention on students who were in danger of failing. But focusing attention was only half the battle. The other half was the iron-willed determination of the advisor/mentor to not let any student in his or her advisory fail. The advisor would not let excuses keep anyone from their responsibilities. The advisor could not afford the luxury of pointing fingers of blame at out-of-school factors or at the students themselves. Students glided through space in their own capsules, and the only thing preventing them from tragedy, from not getting safely to the destination awaiting them in their future, was the advisor.

The Big W was what made "failure is not an option" operational. The Big W was work, as in "the thing you have to do if you want to succeed is work." All of the school-of-life activities, all of the miniconferences, all of the mentoring, and all of the fun were for one purpose: to focus on and support students in working hard. The Big W was the equalizer, the thing that leveled socioeconomic status and race. Work was the biggest school-of-life lesson of all.

The third piece, advisory as family, was just a restatement of the three-plus-one model: teachers needed to treat their advisees as if they were their own kids, tracking and coaching them to success. I can tell you that my advisory mirrored my own family in the joys and the sorrows that it brought me. Not every day was a good day, like when I found myself having to get after Carlos (again!) or when I had to tell a student that he had to go to alternative school. I experienced both sadness and relief when one student asked me to switch to another advisor because "you're always putting pressure on me." I counseled my students. I worked hard to understand where they were coming from. I scolded them. And, yes, I loved them.

The payoff? I got to see the Diego brothers, who came to us from Mexico as a freshman and a sophomore and spoke no English, not only graduate, but also pass the reading and writing portions of our state test—in English. They didn't do it until their senior year, but they did it. I also got to see Amada, who knew that her sister was smarter than she was, who knew that her parents thought she was not very bright, and who qualified for special education, pass her state tests (also in her senior year). The look on her face when she learned her results will stay with me forever because I saw that a life had been changed. I watched these students, and every one of the students in my advisory, graduate.

To that end, I would like to close this chapter with a quote from Johann Wolfgang von Goethe, which famed NFL coach Jimmy Johnson paraphrases: "Treat a person as he is, and he will remain as he is. Treat a person as if he were where he could be and should be, and he will become what he could be and should be."

Chapter 5

OUR READING INTERVENTION

This chapter contains an in-depth look at our special reading intervention. We think it is critical that all readers understand what made our approaches so effective with struggling high school readers. These approaches, detailed in the first half of the chapter, hold the key to improving effectiveness with all students. The second half of the chapter delves into the details of our successful literacy intervention.

An All-Too-Common Story

Several years after we put our advisory program in place, we went to our middle school late in the spring to do a welcome-to-our-high-school orientation for the freshmen-to-be. With me were the four staff members who would serve as the students' advisors/mentors for the next four years. Although school reform had been in progress in our district for years, middle school students were still coming to us with very low reading scores. Simply doing what they had always done up to that point was not going to be enough, and the students needed to know it.

Following the orientation, we set up conferences with each family and the student's advisor. I scheduled appointments, too, because I was filling in for a teacher who could not attend the special day. I can still remember when Fernanda came in with her family. Everyone was all smiles. I was smiling, too. It is not often you get both parents to attend a conference. Unfortunately, the family was in for a big shock.

After a few minutes of pleasantries, we started talking about the reason for our conference. "One thing that is different about going to high school," I explained, "is that your grades matter a lot more than in middle school. Not only do you want to get good grades so you can go on to a college or trade school after high school, but you also have to pass your classes or you can't graduate. How have you been doing in your classes at the middle school, Fernanda? Have you been passing them?"

"Yes, Mister," she answered.

I pulled out her transcript. She was right; it contained mostly Bs and Cs. Not great, but she was definitely passing all her classes. Her parents beamed with pride. They knew that Fernanda was going to be the first in her family to graduate from high school. Then I turned to the next page in her folder. Uh-oh.

"Fernanda, do you like to read?" I asked. She admitted that she did not much care for it.

"Do you know what your reading level is?" Here she fidgeted a bit, before saying she did not. I pulled out her reading test score sheet to lay out the evidence in front of everyone.

"Your reading level is a four point five," I told her. "That means you are reading at the level of someone who is in the fourth grade." Looks of shock and disbelief came over her parents' faces. Fernanda looked down, embarrassed.

"How can this be, Mr. Esparza?" her parents asked. "How can she be reading like a fourth grader when she's in the eighth grade? She gets good grades. You said so yourself. She always does her work."

I looked at Fernanda; she had tears in her eyes. I looked at her parents; they were riding an ocean surging with hurt, anger, shame, and confusion. I felt frustrated that I could not do anything about the past, but pointing fingers of blame was not going to do any good. It was simply time to plan for a better future.

I explained that Fernanda was not alone; I had seen a lot of students like her. She did not like to read because reading was hard for her. That meant that she had made a habit of avoiding reading, and so she had missed out on a lot of practice, practice that was necessary to become a good high school reader. Fortunately for Fernanda, we knew what to do about it. I told the family that we had a program that would make it easier for Fernanda to read, but we needed their help. Fernanda needed to promise to read thirty to sixty minutes per day, and her parents had to promise to help her stick to it.

"If you do that, I promise we'll do our part to make reading easier for you. You're going to make it, Fernanda," I added. "You're going to make it if you really want it and work hard for it." Fernanda looked up, her eyes searching mine. She did not believe me yet. "You do your part," I said with every ounce of conviction I could show, "and we'll do ours. I promise."

A few years earlier, I would not have been so certain.

A Classroom Full of Fernandas

In my first semester at Granger High School, when the staff and I were in the midst of the evaluation conflagration (see chapter 2), one of the first evaluations

I did was in a freshman English class. The teacher was a lifetime resident of the area who had started teaching in our school a few years earlier, after her own children were of school age. Her love for students was undeniable. Her energy as she taught a lesson on *Romeo and Juliet* was unflagging. But the look on many of her students' faces was unmistakable: utter apathy.

Later that day, she and I sat down to debrief. I complimented her energy and her passion for both her subject and her students. Then I brought up what had to be brought up for the sake of our students. "I looked up the current grades of your students in that class. I saw that eighteen out of twenty-one are failing. That is unacceptable," I said.

Instead of making excuses, instead of angrily blaming the students or shaking a finger at me, she visibly relaxed. "I'm glad you noticed," she said. "I've been doing everything I can think of, and they're just not making it. They struggle so much with reading, and I have no idea what to do. None of my classes ever taught me how to be a reading teacher to high school kids."

What she described was a systemic problem. Our original system was not designed to handle large numbers of secondary students who did not read well. Yes, it would have been nice if we could just say, "They should have learned that in elementary school," but what good would that do? We needed to be realistic and give our teachers help with this problem. They were the ones who were faced with trying to make progress with kids who had built up a resistance to anything reading-related. That resistance turned a hard job into an impossible job. Attitudes and beliefs hardened and turned negative, first for students and then for teachers when they saw their lack of ability to effect change. If we were going to help our students, we had to help our teachers, too. We had to give them new strategies and systemic changes that would help them break through their limiting beliefs and aim higher.

As I listened to this teacher, as I saw her frustration and thought about all those failing kids, I had an idea. I had met Will Roulston the previous year, when he explained Second Shot Reading, a locally developed reading intervention, to me. The goal of the program was to turn around discouraged, struggling teenage readers and build up not just their skills in reading, but also their confidence as learners. The needs of our students—and our frustrated teachers—were so strong that I was willing to risk starting a new pilot program in the middle of my first year. If it worked, it would give the kids a huge boost, and the eventual payoff in staff morale would be tremendous.

Data Points: Before and After Intervention

Our students took the WASL exams in the spring of their fourth-, seventh-, and tenth-grade years to test their proficiency. The data showed that only 2 percent of our students had passed the reading and writing sections of the WASL as seventh graders, which meant that 98 percent of the students in the freshman English class were reading below standard. The reading portion of the WASL (since modified and retitled "High School Proficiency Exam") measured reading comprehension on fiction and nonfiction texts.

As part of the test, students had to read and answer questions (multiple-choice, short response, and essays) about several articles that were two to four pages in length. A sampling of the learning targets that students had to complete follows:

- Demonstrate understanding of theme or message and supportive details

- Make inferences or predictions

- Make generalizations beyond the text to a broader idea or concept

- Analyze author's purpose and evaluate effectiveness for different audiences (including fact/opinion, author's point of view, tone, and use of persuasive devices)

- Interpret general and specialized vocabulary critical to the meaning of the text

- Apply understanding of literary elements (genres; story elements such as plot, character, setting, stylistic devices) and graphic elements/illustrations

- Summarize text

- Compare/contrast elements of the text or make connections within the text

- Apply understanding of text features (titles, headings, and other information divisions, tables of contents, indexes, glossaries, prefaces, appendices, captions) (Office of Superintendent of Public Instruction, 2001)

This daunting list of tasks was so challenging that parents and community groups all over the state led revolts, saying that the test was too hard, especially for our poor and minority students.

Will and I fully supported the high standards of the WASL in reading. We knew that high-stakes testing would inevitably cause teachers to teach to the test. That is not a problem if the test is a good one, and we knew the WASL, at least at the tenth-grade level, measured real-world skills that we wanted all our students to have. If they could pass the WASL, they would have the reading, writing, and thinking foundation to learn to do anything they wanted in life.

The WASL used four levels to describe student performance, as shown in table 5.1.

Table 5.1: Proficiency Levels on the WASL Reading Exam

Proficiency Level	Descriptor	Relation to Standard
Level 4	Advanced	Meets standard
Level 3	Proficient	Meets standard
Level 2	Basic	Below standard
Level 1	Below basic	Below standard

Ninety-eight percent of our first year's freshman class scored below standard when they were seventh graders, and 56 percent tested at level 1, below basic. No wonder we saw so much anger and frustration in our students and teachers. I looked at this data with the freshman English teacher in December 1999 and realized that time was short. We had just thirteen months of classroom instruction before those freshmen had to take the WASL in April of their sophomore year.

In the spring semester of the 1999–2000 school year, we piloted Second Shot Reading successfully in one classroom. It soon became our main intervention to get our students reading, writing, and thinking proficiently. In the ensuing years, Will continued to refine it, eventually retitling it Rewire Reading to incorporate the advances.

How successful was it? In April 2001, those incoming freshmen from my first year—the class of 2003—took their tenth-grade WASL. They scored only 20 percent proficient in reading and 11 percent in writing. Although we were discouraged, we realized that the students had made huge leaps over their scores in the seventh grade. In fact, where 56 percent of them scored below basic in reading in the seventh grade, only 32 percent were still below basic. We were trending upward. And we built more and more success in the following years, even though the students were still coming to us with very low proficiency scores from our elementary and middle schools. Figure 5.1 (page 90) shows the reading scores for our students for their fourth-, seventh-, and tenth-grade years.

As shown in figure 5.1, our high schoolers made steady progress, even though we had only about fifteen months (from the time they entered school in September until the test dates in April) of instructional time to get ready for the WASL. Look, for example, at the class of 2005. As fourth-graders, only 12 percent demonstrated fourth-grade-level proficiency. When they were seventh-graders trying to meet the more-challenging seventh-grade standards, only 11 percent were able to do it. As sophomores, 38 percent of these same students demonstrated proficiency on the higher standards of the tenth-grade test. Although the elementary and middle schools started to make some progress eventually, the amount of growth between students' seventh- and tenth-grade years showed that what we were doing was working.

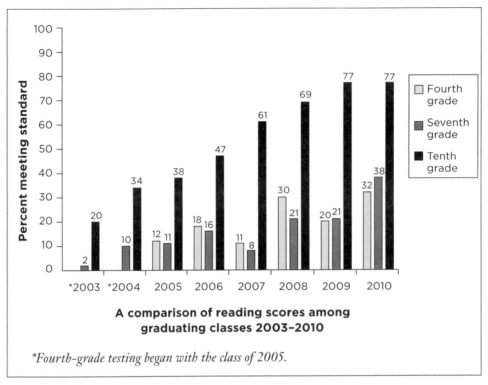

Figure 5.1: Improvement in our students' WASL reading scores over the years.

Perhaps a better measure of effectiveness is to look at our scores compared to the average passing rate of all students in Washington over the same time period (see fig. 5.2). The results show that although there was general improvement for all students taking the test, our students improved at a much faster rate. Remember our demographics: 90 percent free and reduced lunch and 90 percent students of color. By the time the class of 2007 took the WASL in the spring of 2009, they were performing at nearly the same level as the average of all students in our state. We had effectively closed the achievement gap in reading.

The story in writing proficiency (see fig. 5.3) looks fairly similar to our reading improvement. After several years of rapid growth, we seemed to level off at 67 percent of our sophomores meeting standard in writing, still a sizable increase from their earlier performance. Although we continued to implement more interventions aimed at writing in subsequent years, the summary writing part of the Rewire Reading curriculum was the one constant intervention aimed at writing through all the years represented on the graph shown in figure 5.3.

Another result of our Rewire intervention was classroom teachers reporting that students were approaching reading and writing with more confidence. Some reported that students would volunteer to read aloud in front of the whole class— a significant breakthrough for students who had been cowed into silence for so

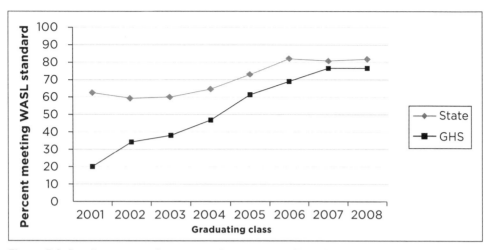

Figure 5.2: Reading scores: Granger students versus all students in Washington.

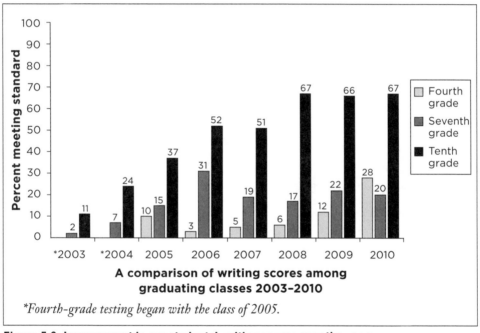

Figure 5.3: Improvement in our students' writing scores over the years.

many years because of their reading disability. Other teachers noted that Rewire students involved in group projects, especially ones that required reading, were participating more in the activities than they had previously. Still other teachers reported that when students had to read individually in class, they would get right to it, tracking all the way.

Our results go against the interpretation of research made by Kati Haycock of the Education Trust. Haycock's research showed that a student who has two ineffective teachers in successive years will lose so much educational ground that he or she may never recover (as quoted in Rapides Foundation, 2006). Although I advocate for early intervention—and the earlier, the better—our results lead me to say that we can never give up on our struggling high school students. It is never too late to turn around reading.

Our Readers

Are struggling adolescent readers different from struggling younger readers? Absolutely. Things get a lot more complicated by the time students reach high school. Our kids were scarred by previous failures, and their failures had led them over the years to adopt negative beliefs, attitudes, and habits. If we did not deal with those realities, our interventions would fail.

Bad Beliefs, Bad Attitudes, and Bad Habits

We needed to change our students' negative belief systems. Time and again, in education and in the world at large, I have seen the influence of belief on people's behavior. When people think they cannot do something, they do not approach it with confidence, and they usually do not succeed—that is, if they even try at all. Our students felt like failures because they did not learn to read as easily as other kids. We had to prove to them that they were not failures. They were not dumb; they just were not developmentally ready when they first learned to read, or the instruction did not match the way they learned best. We needed to show our students that if they worked with us, putting in as much effort as we were willing to put in to help them, they could turn it around.

Our students had developed negative attitudes about reading and school as a defense mechanism against the boredom of reading that did not make sense. These negative beliefs and attitudes had, over time, formed into negative habits that we needed to break down and re-form into positive habits. The struggling readers habitually approached reading differently from the way good readers approached text. Their powers of concentration were lacking because reading was a seriously boring exercise of sounding out words. Their brains were not actively engaged in making meaning because they had nine years of practice in mouthing words and going through the motions.

We needed strategic methods to teach these students to engage at a high level, seeking meaning from text, questioning it, and finding pleasure in the process. These methods also had to keep students interested enough to use these new behaviors consistently over a long enough period of time that they developed totally new habits. If they were going to succeed in erasing the achievement gap, we needed to help them experience literacy that was powerful and pleasurable.

Parrot Responses

Our students reflected the homes they had grown up in. Researchers like Grover Whitehurst (1997) have documented the simplified vocabulary and nonstandard grammar of children reared in poverty. Because our students had weak language skills, they dutifully learned to be good parrots in the early grades. They read the words of their reading lesson aloud, and when the teacher corrected their pronunciation, they mimicked her the best they could. But more often than not, it was assumed that students knew the meaning of a large number of words because they could say those words aloud. They *seemed* to be reading, but the students didn't understand the *meaning* of what they were reading. They were simply responding like parrots, and their comprehension was about the same as a parrot's understanding of English or any other language.

So we worked with these students not only to develop their vocabularies, but also to break the bad habit of reading without engaging their brains in making sense of what they were reading. Our students needed to learn to stop and ask questions anytime something did not make sense, or they would be forever stuck with substandard language and reading skills. Easier said than done with teenagers who do not want to expose what they do not know after years of pretending they did know.

Turning Around Struggling Adolescent Readers

Students who are not good at reading avoid it like the plague. They have plenty of excuses: reading is boring; reading is for schoolboys; I don't need to be able to read, I'll just wait for the movie. Underneath all these excuses is simple avoidance behavior.

Any reading intervention worth pursuing must use strategies that tackle these avoidance behaviors. Inside these big bodies are just scared little kids, afraid to fail one more time. Like parents, we have to introduce them to ways they can be successful and support them through the transition. Sometimes we guide them with firmness, sometimes with empathy, but always with the knowledge that their psyches have been bruised. Those bruises are a major factor that keeps struggling students from fully engaging in the process of turning around their reading skills. If we can take away the fear, they can soar.

Fluency

Fluency means that the act of decoding letters into sounds, sounds into words, and words into sentences has become automatic. The focus of students' attention no longer has to be on sounding out individual words; instead, they can focus their attention on understanding what the author is saying. If students find intrigue in the tales that authors tell or their brains light up when they learn new information, they will like reading. Students who like reading will read.

Students with poor fluency remain stuck in a halting, hesitating form of recognizing individual words. Their experience when reading is like the experience you have when you head to another room in your house to retrieve your sunglasses before you go outside. Along the way, you notice that someone left the milk out, so you stop to put it in the refrigerator. Then you notice that someone actually spilled milk on the counter, and when you reach for the paper towels, you realize you are out of them. So you grab a pen to start a shopping list, but the pen does not work, so you go searching for another. By the time you find a pen that works, you have been bombarded by so many different thoughts as you looked around the house that you will be lucky if you remember what to write down, let alone that you need to clean up the milk or that you were originally going to get your sunglasses. You might not even remember until later, when you are paying bills, that you intended to go outside at all. Students who are not fluent see individual words like individual tasks. They work on one word, and by the time they have finished working on the next one, they have forgotten what they read before. They read a sentence like a list of words, not seeing the connections, not hearing the author's voice.

The easiest way to tell if students have reading problems is to ask them to read aloud. Fluent reading sounds smooth. It flows easily because students understand what they are reading. Some definitions of fluency define it only in terms of accuracy and rate; it can be measured as the number of words read correctly per minute. Many high school readers read quickly and pronounce words correctly, yet they do so with a flat tone that sounds like the early computer voices of the 1990s. Their disembodied voices reflect that they do not understand what they are reading. You can recognize fluent reading because it sounds much like students are speaking their own words when they read aloud.

Most students who aren't fluent don't like reading. We liken the reading experience of good readers and poor readers to watching movies. Fluent readers can make movies when they read, movies as exciting as any 3-D blockbuster at an IMAX theater. Poor readers, however, sit in a dark theater with no picture and no sound, just the smell of burnt popcorn and the sticky floors from spilled sodas. Because poor readers do not like reading, they do not read in their free time, and this lack of reading locks these students into a cycle of failure. Because they do not read, they are not exposed to new vocabulary words and new ways of putting words together into more complex and elegant sentences. They are not exposed to new ideas and knowledge that good readers are exposed to, and they end up with less background knowledge. When the reading material in school gets more difficult, they are not able to keep up.

This scenario is the same one that Fernanda, the student you met at the beginning of this chapter, experienced. Because she was not able to read fluently with understanding, she stopped reading outside of school. She was able to keep up with her middle school classes because of her superior work ethic. But she was headed for a lot of struggle in high school, as the reading became more demanding. The good readers in her class were like Milo of Croton, who was able to lift a full-grown bull on his shoulders because he had started carrying it when it was a calf and kept carrying it every day as it got progressively heavier. Good readers developed the skills to do the heavy lifting of high school reading over time. Some of this skill was due to the direct teaching of vocabulary and English grammar, but a large portion came through frequent contact with more advanced, academic language while reading.

Interest

As many different reasons as there are to read, it all boils down to two: people read for pleasure and/or power. Avid readers devour text because they like it. Other highly skilled readers may not rank reading as one of their favorite hobbies, but when they do read, they seek out information they can use, information that helps them at work or helps them to solve a problem or make better choices in their personal lives. In short, they derive power from reading.

We believed that if we could make our students more fluent and show them that reading could be easier, more meaningful, and more interesting, we could make it easier for them to read more. If they would take the next step and choose to read more, then they could break the failure cycle and change it into a success cycle.

Overall, we had a good idea of why our kids were struggling; we had strong beliefs about what they needed in order to make a turnaround; and we had a locally developed program that we thought was perfect.

The Rewire Reading Setup

Will stumbled onto the beginnings of our reading intervention in his job as a curriculum generalist with the Migrant Education Regional Office in Yakima, Washington. One day, he was invited to observe a pilot project in a middle school Title I reading classroom in Pasco, Washington. He was amazed by what long-time teacher Ruth Cole had created. Never had he seen a classroom of so many struggling readers so deeply engaged in learning to read and write. When year-end test results were in, they matched his anecdotal observations of the impact the program was having.

Together, Will and Ruth planned to try to disseminate her strategy to nine school districts the next year. Unfortunately, Ruth had heart surgery during the summer and died as a result of complications. Not willing to let Ruth's work pass away with her, Will worked with the three paraeducators Ruth had trained and put together a training program based on their reflections and his own research. The pilot program went on as scheduled; the nine districts experienced great success, and Will continued to experiment and refine his approaches as other schools asked for his help. Now, in December 1999, I was asking him to help us put together our pilot program to turn around our struggling readers.

Training

The training to get started consisted of two full days, during which Will trained the freshman English teacher and her aides, which was critical.

Richard Allington (2002), in a section of his book *Big Brother and the National Reading Curriculum* titled "No Such Thing as a Proven Program," cites a large-scale evaluation of commercial elementary reading programs (including some that are popular today) in which the evaluators found that no program worked well at all sites. He concluded, "If the concentrated effort of highly competent and well-funded sponsors with a few sites cannot produce uniform results from locality to locality, it seems doubtful that any model program could" (House, Glass, McLean, & Walker, 1978, p. 154). Allington (2002) commented that their conclusion was "the one consistent finding in educational research: Programs don't teach, teachers do" (p. 17). In accordance with this belief, Rewire is successful only inasmuch as the teachers' and paraeducators' commitments to follow the training and become more skilled at using the model to teach reading.

Ruth Cole led by example during the year she was developing her program in her classroom. Because her school used a pullout model for serving students, she and her three aides worked with students four days a week and used Fridays to prepare for the coming week and to review what had happened that week. They were a true *professional learning community* before that term was in vogue.

We were unable to use a pullout model, and thus we couldn't provide that kind of ongoing training built into the schedule for Rewire. Still, we tried not to lose sight of the need for ongoing reflection that would allow our practitioners to refine their understanding of Rewire Reading, observe the progress of their students, and adapt their practices to ensure higher student success. These reflection times were sometimes stolen from our weekly staff-development times or our professional development days for teachers, when all teachers were supposed to be working on the same thing or listening to the same presentation. I had to be up front with the rest of my staff and tell them that because reading was such a huge need, I was releasing the Rewire teachers to work together.

Staffing

As we describe in chapter 6, once we adopted Rewire as our primary intervention, we used it in our English 1 and 2 classes for students who were two or more years below grade level in reading. Within a class, we divided our students into homogenous groups by reading levels, with each group consisting of four to five students. We limited these reading-focused English classes to twenty students, and we had three to four paraeducators or volunteers in addition to the teacher in the classroom.

How did we get so many paraeducators? Like many schools, we already had them, hired with money from the Title I program, the migrant program, or special education. Getting their help with the Rewire program was a simple matter of focusing their services on the most critical need of these students, which we determined was reading, just as it was for many of our other students. If a special education student was mainstreamed into our reading class, for example, it made perfect sense for a special education paraeducator to come into the reading class for the first thirty minutes and help the student, not only with his or her reading, but also with his or her interaction with the other students while everyone participated in the same learning activity. After Rewire was finished, the tutor headed back to the special education classroom or out into another classroom where students were being mainstreamed. The same scenario repeated with the tutors that we paid through other programs.

We faced administrative pressure from district officials for this choice. They did not want to allow categorically funded paraeducators to deliver services to students who were not funded by their particular program. For example, their stance was that if the bilingual program funded the paraeducator, that paraeducator could not give instruction to nonbilingual students. Our interpretation was that the paraeducators were there to help the specific students for which they received funding, and if the best way to help these students was to participate in an activity, such as Rewire, with other students, then that method was serving the best interest of the student. We challenged district administrators: would you really like the migrant student to stop receiving small-group, Rewire Reading instruction just because other students are being helped? We argued that small-group interaction was the best setting for these students to learn in, offering benefits far beyond one-on-one tutoring. Although the administrators still were not thrilled with what we were doing, they could not in good faith argue that they wanted us to stop serving the students. State monitors finally settled the matter when they came to visit; they agreed that we were in full compliance with their understanding of the laws.

Placement

We grouped our students for instruction according to reading level—first grade, second grade, third grade, and so on—based on two or three data points. The student's reading comprehension level score from the Gates-MacGinitie test was one data point. Then we tested students' reading rate one-on-one by using leveled reading passages that we took from our reading materials. We selected the leveled reading passage that was closest to their Gates-MacGinitie score. We asked them to read aloud for one minute, advising them not to read so fast that they would not comprehend the text because we would ask them to talk about the story when finished. If a student read the passage at a rate of about 80–100 words per minute, we usually placed him or her at that level. If a student read faster than that, yet showed little recall of what was read, we figured that same level was also a good level at which to start. Such students were good at what some have called "barking at print"; they may have been making noises, but they weren't making sense. If a student read slower than 80 words, we retested him or her with a lower-level passage, and if the student read faster than 100 and wasn't just barking words, we retested him or her with a higher-level passage. With high school students who had received remedial reading instruction, we often found that they could read at 120–200 words per minute, but they had so little comprehension that we thought it best to start them at their reading comprehension level so they could refocus their attention on making sense while they were reading.

Preparing the Materials

The materials we used in our Rewire program were the same ones that Ruth Cole used. They were old, reproducible stories published by Turman Publishing Company. Each story was really a nonfiction article about a topic: mysterious events, interesting people, or animals and nature. The articles were meant to be highly engaging to unenthusiastic readers. We wanted tutors and students alike to enjoy learning new things and to make personal connections to the content in the stories while talking about them.

Turman published its articles by grade level: 2.5, 3.0, 3.5, and so forth. If we could engage our students in making meaning of the articles they read at their current level, they would be preparing themselves for more advanced reading. As the reading level of the articles increased, vocabulary grew in difficulty and quantity, and the syntax of the sentences became increasingly more complex. The end result was a reader like Milo of Croton hoisting his ever-larger bull: the student grew stronger vocabulary and language skills and was able to comprehend increasingly more complex text.

Because the Turman materials began at a 2.5 grade level, and because we had readers testing below that level, Will wrote new articles that started at the 1.0

level so that we could use them with our most challenged students, typically our new English learners and special education students. He made sure that the content was age-appropriate so our students didn't feel that what they had to read was babyish and demeaning. He also wrote new material for seventh- and eighth-grade levels to make sure we could take students all the way up to high school level.

Each article had a running total of the number of words printed discreetly at the beginning of each line, which helped us with the timing portions of the Rewire Reading program.

The Schedule

Rewire followed a structured schedule (see fig. 5.4).

---

1. Write summary of yesterday's article.

2. Participate in first "prewired" timing on today's article.

3. Pay attention as article is modeled three times by tutor.

4. Reread article three to five times.

5. Participate in second "rewired" timing on article.

6. Answer questions from article.

7. Chart your results.

8. Finish/revise summary.

Figure 5.4: Rewire Reading schedule.

One of the secrets to working with discouraged students is to use positive inertia. We know that a body at rest will remain at rest until acted on by an outside force, and the Rewire schedule served as the force that pushed our students out of their apathetic, slow-moving, body-at-rest inertia.

The schedule of Rewire activities was to be completed in twenty-five to thirty minutes. For this to be possible, students had to begin working on their summaries as soon as they entered the classroom. We explained to them that this prompt action was nonnegotiable. We role-played how they were expected to come in quietly, without disturbing anyone else, and quickly get to work before the bell rang. This process took some reinforcement and directives to "try again," but soon they began to do it automatically. They had only about five minutes to write the summary, so they learned that if they did not do it immediately, they would not be able to successfully complete everything.

By using this process, we changed their negative inertia of slogging slowly through their school day into positive inertia by getting them fully engaged in fast-paced learning. And just as a body in motion will remain in motion until it is acted on by an outside force, once we had those bodies moving, the rapid pace of the schedule kept them moving rapidly. If the schedule slowed, so did the students, back to the pace they usually moved at, which was something we definitely did not want. Overcoming their old heel-dragging inertia was critical in changing their attitudes and creating a new habit of focused attention to their work. We wanted students to get very good at being able to focus all their energy on the task of learning. We hoped that if they enjoyed the feelings, not only of success, but also the joy in the process of working hard, they would carry this attitude into the rest of their school day.

Rewire Step-by-Step

What follows is a step-by-step explanation of how we taught Rewire at Granger. The practices described here are the basic strategies that we emphasized with all tutors.

Step 1: Summary Writing

As the first task in the Rewire Reading schedule, we required students to write a summary of the article they had read and discussed in the previous Rewire session, not the new article they would read later in the session. As students entered the class, they first picked up their folder of materials, a Pee Chee–style folder containing a chart of their progress and a number of recently read articles. The most recent article was kept in the left pocket, just in front of the chart. The other articles were kept in the right pocket. This organization made it easy to find the article needed for writing the summary. With folders in hand, the students moved to their desks (already arranged in clusters for each group before the students arrived), took out their papers and pens, and started to write.

The articles were photocopied on one side of a piece of paper, with the back side either left blank or lined like ruled paper to make writing easier. When students needed to refer to the article to refresh their memory or look up the spelling of a word that was in the article, it was a simple matter of flipping over the paper.

It's important to understand both the difficulty and the importance of summary writing. (Step 6 details the elements of summary writing that we worked on with the students.) If reading is difficult for struggling students, writing is just as difficult for most. To read, students have to decode the letters into recognizable words and string the words together into sentences that express thoughts. To write, they must encode thoughts and words into letters on paper. If students can't figure out how to decode a word when reading it—a process for which they have the advantage of using sentence context to help them figure out what it might be—they won't be able to encode it correctly when writing it. Context can't help; they simply have to know how it's spelled. Learning to write words correctly, therefore, is important and can actually help make learning to read them easier. The act of encoding (writing down the words) reinforces the decoding work (reading the words) they did when they read the article the day before. The practice of encoding has advantages over decoding for teaching reading because it slows down the process and helps students notice how words are constructed. Think about it: students can write only one letter at a time. The process of writing a letter takes longer than just looking at a letter. So writing slows students down and forces them to pay attention to each letter of the word.

Another advantage that writing text has over simply reading it is that writing is kinesthetic. In fact, if iterative writing (see step 3)—a practice we advocate for words and spelling patterns that trouble the student— is done, then we have turned a very sedentary activity into a multisensory, active one. Instead of just seeing with their eyes and thinking silently in their heads, students are seeing, thinking, saying, hearing, and using their hands in concert with their brains to produce text. Brilliant!

The summaries consisted of a topic sentence that stated the main idea of the article and followed up with three to six sentences that elaborated the other main ideas or supportive details. Think for a moment about what cognitive skills students need to do this well: the ability to distinguish between main ideas and details, the ability to group details and construct the underlying main idea they add up to, and the ability to differentiate between important details and trivial ones. Then students must reverse the process and put these ordered bits—main idea and details—back together on paper so that each sentence connects to the ones above it and flows to the next. Many high school sophomores still have not perfected this ability, yet this is exactly the kind of high-level thinking our students needed to be able to do to pass our state reading and writing tests and, more important, to prepare for college or highly skilled jobs. Summary writing was one of the most important skills we could work on. It really gave maximum results for our instructional efforts.

Because summary writing is difficult, the students struggled with it at first. Our key to success was to focus on the work before us each day, trying to improve only one or two elements of each student's summary, trusting that as long as we kept them working, they would improve. Have you heard the old joke asking, "How do you eat an elephant?" We tackled the problem of teaching summaries in the same way: "One bite at a time."

Step 2: First Timing

As students worked on their summaries, the tutor for the group, seated at a desk a short distance away, called over one student at a time for testing. The tutor gave the student a copy of a new passage to read aloud for one minute. While the student read, the tutor used a highlighter pen to mark any errors on a second copy of the same article. When the timer went off at the one-minute mark, the tutor counted the number of words read correctly and wrote the number on the top of the copy along with the student's name. The student then returned to his or her desk to continue working on the article summary, and the next student met with the tutor for first timing. This student read from a clean copy of the article while the tutor marked errors and total words read correctly on another copy. This process was rapidly repeated so all students could be timed before any of them finished writing their summary. Once we had students engaged with summary writing, we wanted the tyranny of the schedule to keep them moving along at such a fast pace that they could not disengage. With all the timings completed, the tutor would move to the cluster of desks where the students were sitting and get ready for the next step.

Step 3: Modeled Reading

Other than the fast-paced schedule that creates a high level of engagement, modeled reading is the most important variable in the Rewire program. Will believes that modeling excellent reading for struggling readers will work faster than any other strategy to demystify the reading process. A computer cannot replicate modeling reading any more than it could successfully raise a child. Computers run off scripts and can be programmed to do some pretty complex functions, but if the computers need to do something that deviates from the preprogrammed script, they don't know how to respond. Modeling simplifies an extremely complex instructional task.

Struggling readers are each unique in their blend of strengths, weaknesses, skills, knowledge, experiences, personality, and emotions. If those variables are not a big enough challenge, add the interaction among these diverse students in a group and the fact that their moods fluctuate daily, especially as teenagers.

Will likes to relay the story another teacher told him about her son's aeronautics class at the University of Washington. On the first day of class, the professor announced that the students' grades would be based primarily on a quarter-long project. They would do the calculations for how to successfully launch a satellite, make it do a specified number of revolutions around the Earth and perform certain functions, and then safely reenter the atmosphere and land. The professor also explained that students would complete the project in groups of three, which he would assign. Immediately, several hands went up in the class, all to ask the same question: "What if I don't want to work in a group? I'd rather work alone." The professor told the students that they could work by themselves if they chose, but if they chose that route, they would most likely fail, because this really was rocket science. The problems the students would encounter were just too complex for any one person to handle alone. Despite this warning, some of the students chose to work on the project on their own. At the end of the quarter when the grades were revealed, the professor's prophecy was proven true. Each student who worked in a group had managed to successfully complete the project; each student who worked alone had failed it.

The teacher who told Will this tale thought that the moral of the story was that we all need to work together on very complex activities, and that is certainly true. But Will likes to point out something else: those students had it a lot easier than any classroom teacher. After all, there are laws of physics that reliably describe that when you do A, B will occur every time. Based on that law, you can look up formulas, plug in the math, and do rocket science. But what law of human nature states that every time you do X or Y to a student, the result is Z? Teachers, in essence, have thirty different rockets in their classroom, each one slightly different from the other. Teachers should be so lucky to have it as easy as rocket scientists!

To deal with so much complexity, Rewire uses the two most powerful learning technologies in the world: modeling and conversation. The overview of the process is this: the tutor reads the article aloud three times, discussing vocabulary and confusing elements, and making connections to students' existing knowledge. And the tutor does all of this while maintaining a rapid pace that keeps up the momentum established earlier. It is quite a juggling act.

The Modeled Reading Process

After all the first timings were done, the tutor moved to the students' cluster of desks and asked the students to put their summaries in their folders. She then handed them their copy of the daily reading, the one on which she had marked their errors with a highlighter. When all students had their "tracker" ready, she began the first read-through. The *tracker* was the index finger that students used to trace under the words as they followed along. Some reading teachers consider this a babyish practice that slows down readers. In our experience, the tracker was a useful tool that helped students focus their attention by making reading more active and multisensory. Will demonstrated to students that he used his tracker when he was reading in a noisy room or at times when he just could not concentrate, but he also showed them how when he was having no trouble reading, he didn't need to use it. That made pretty good sense to the students; they'd use it as a transition strategy to get good and use it only when they needed it thereafter.

The tutor conducted her first read-through with good expression that emphasized the meaning of the text, modeling good reading, the first of our two powerful technologies. Will uses an analogy he learned while studying to be a track coach to paint a picture of why he believes modeling is such a powerful technology. The analogy comes from the secret of how coaches trained Russian sprinters to be some of the fastest in the world by using a method called "over-speed train-ing." One such method is to run downhill, but the other method, the one Will emphasizes, is to put a belt on the sprinter and attach a rope, which is attached to a motorcycle, to the sprinter's belt. The coach then gets on the motorcycle, and as he starts to accelerate down the track, the sprinter starts to run with it. When the sprinter reaches his top speed, the coach accelerates the motorcycle just a little bit more. The sprinter is literally pulled along at a speed faster than he could accomplish on his own. After training like this for a while, the sprint-er's speed actually increases. His nervous system has been trained to fire faster. In one sense, this is what modeled reading does for students. This method takes their stumbling, bumbling, decoding-each-word-with-effort reading pace and pulls them along faster than they can go on their own, breaking habits and form-ing new, faster neural pathways.

Because we did not want to train parrots that simply repeat words, it was criti-cal that the tutor stopped frequently during the first read-through to clarify and connect to the text instead of just reading it to the students straight through. This was where our second powerful learning technology came into play: con-versation. Will has gotten a lot of grief for calling conversation a technology, but think about it. Conversation reveals what another person is thinking. It reveals misunderstandings or gaps in knowledge, not by the taking and grading of a test, but by the simple act of conversing. Conversation allows teachers to give help at the point of need—at the moment their students need it, not at the moment the script predicted they would need help. Conversation is evidence-based, respond-ing to the needs students reveal, not based on our assumptions of what they need.

Consider the following example of a modeled reading conversation. Is there any other learning technology—computer program, scripted learning program, video- or web-based presentation—that can so efficiently and effectively engage students in learning?

During the first read-through, the tutor asked the students, "What's another word for *strapping*?" She listened to the answers and responded. There was no script we could give her that would cover all variables of the text and what stu-dents already knew or what information or skills they lacked. The questions and opportunities for conversation came from the need to make sense of and con-nect to what the author was saying. The tutor pointed out that the word *strapping* has multiple meanings when the students started talking about tape for mailing packages. She explained how in this context *strapping* meant big and strong, as in "a strapping fellow is big and strong." She was asked why *strapping* meant this and realized that she did not know. She wrote down the word, promising to look up the origin later and let the students know. While writing down the word, she thought of the father in the animated film *The Incredibles* and used him as a visual of someone who was strapping.

This is the power of conversation. There was no stopping for drills or to look up information, just the sharing of information to clarify and increase connections to the topic at hand. At just the right time, at the moment when the information was needed to clarify something, the good reader shared something the text brought to her mind. But it wasn't one-way teaching as much as it was a two-way dialogue.

One of the students, a basketball enthusiast, responded, "Like LeBron James. He's built." Another student said that his uncle Carlos was huge and actually kind of scary because he had a bad attitude, especially when he had been drinking. The tutor was then able to share that *strapping* only had to do with the size and strength of a person; it did not mean that the person was scary or had a bad attitude or drinking problem. As the students read through the rest of the story, they had vivid images in their minds of what it meant to be strapping because the tutor had tied into their prior knowledge. The students were not nearly as likely to forget what *strapping* meant as they might have been had they learned the definition on a worksheet for a test. They would not forget LeBron or Uncle Carlos anytime soon, and *strapping* was now connected to their own personal examples. Their brains were actually functioning like the brain of an excellent reader, pulling information and knowledge from their storehouse of experiences to make the text come alive, making movies in their minds. For maybe the first time ever, the students could follow the conversation that an author was trying to have with them because of the conversation the tutor was having with them while they read.

The tutor did more than ask questions. She shared her own experiences and thoughts as she went. She did what any of us might do when we are reading an interesting article in a magazine or a newspaper and a friend is sitting nearby: we share what we find interesting, funny, or bizarre, or whatever the story makes us think of. The tutor had to be careful not to spend so much time here that the students' attention started to wander, but this practice of reading and conversing was critical. How else could she convince struggling students that reading could be pleasurable and powerful? They had sat so long in the darkened theater of the mind during reading activities that they didn't believe it was possible. We had to let students experience the magic of reading for themselves—repeatedly—by towing them in the wake of a good reader, our tutor, as she interacted authentically with text and helped them to do the same.

By the time the group finished the first read-through, the students had a pretty clear idea of what the article was about. They had clarified the meaning of words and connected them to their prior knowledge. Then the tutor read the article twice more, not stopping as much as the first time through, but instead reading the text in a more connected flow, a little bit faster each time. The students' brains were being towed down the track, with full comprehension, faster than they were able to read on their own. They were breaking poor habits of reading word by word, strengthening their understanding of vocabulary, and absorbing the language patterns of the sentences, which better developed their ear for grammar.

Why We Did Not Focus on Decoding

We did not focus on decoding during our reading instruction. Most of our students had had a lot of decoding practice in other reading interventions over the years, yet they were still not good decoders. So it did not make sense to keep doing the same thing instructionally if we wanted to get different results. Our approach helped students notice how words were spelled by using color to highlight their decoding errors on their papers. Then each time we modeled for them, they connected what they heard to what they saw. We tried to speed up the acquisition of new words through modeling and repetition. Because the brain is an amazing parallel-processing computer, doing many tasks simultaneously, we believed that in most cases this practice was enough to eliminate decoding problems.

Two Writing Strategies That Teach Decoding

In addition to writing summaries, we used two other writing strategies when necessary to make sure students actually noticed the sounds and spellings that made up the words we modeled: similar words and iterative writing.

We asked students to be constantly aware of *similar words*, words that are spelled alike, and to write similar words down. For example, once students learned the word *enough*, it helped them to know that *rough* and *tough* followed the same pattern. Even *slough* fit the pattern, but only when it meant to shed a covering like skin, not when it is a bog or a swamp, in which case *slough* is pronounced like *through*. Is it any wonder that students struggle with phonics lessons when the same letter pattern can also be pronounced like the words *cough*, *bough*, and *dough*? We laughed with the students at the absurdity of it all and admitted that the way English was cobbled together made spelling sometimes confusing.

For our purpose, *iterative writing* meant that students said aloud the sounds of the letters as they wrote them. For example, when writing "enough," the process would be as follows:

1. Write the letter *e*, say "eee" (the long e sound heard in the word *tree*).

2. Write the letter *n*, say "nnn" (not the letter name en-en-en, but the sound you hear at the beginning of the word *no*, holding it out as long as it takes to write the letter).

3. Write the letters *ou*, say "uh."

4. Write the letters *gh*, say "fff."

5. Finish by underlining each syllable, saying the sound each makes while underlining it (underline *e*, saying "e" and then underline *nough* saying "nuff").

We modeled how to do this for students and had them do it with some words, especially those they misspelled in their writing. We also showed them how to sound out the word like it was spelled so that they looked at the word *enough* and said, "EEE-NO-OOH-GUH-HUH." This exercise is just one more way for students to pay attention to the letters and combinations that make up the word, and the novelty of it assists memory.

Step 4: Rereading

When the modeled reading was complete, the students reread the article independently. They read it a minimum of three times, but perhaps as many as five or six times. We asked them to use their tracker so we could watch their progress, see where they were struggling, and offer help. We also wanted them to read in a quiet, whisper voice so they could hear themselves as they read.

Repetition is what turns unpracticed skill into polished skill. If students are reading with full comprehension and with the voice of good reading in their heads as a result of the tutor's read-throughs, then they are building themselves up to a highly proficient reading performance on that short passage, a remarkable achievement in so little time.

Step 5: Second Timing

For the second timings, the tutor moved back to the same place where she did the first timings. As soon as a student was ready, he came to the timing station, bringing the day's article and also the previous day's article with his newly written summary, if he had finished it. The tutor helped with any words the student was still having problems with and then timed him for one minute as he read aloud the same story he had been practicing. She again marked errors, if any, this time using a different-colored highlighter to differentiate errors from first to second timing.

The benefits of Rewire Reading were easy to see, and the improvement of our students was often astounding. Where students might have read 85 words correctly on the first timing, they now read 130, 160, even 190 words per minute. Their attention was usually completely focused on the tutor after the timer went off, waiting to see exactly how much they had improved.

This immediate feedback on their efforts was worth a thousand words of praise. We could tell our students that they were smart all we wanted, but the typical response of discouraged learners was to ignore us. The first several times some students improved on the second timing, they thought they just got lucky because they were so unaccustomed to seeing a payoff for their academic efforts. The repetition drove it home. When students saw results the next day and the day after that and the one after that, they started to believe in the payoff. The success they created from their own efforts turned around their negative beliefs. We gave students the opportunity to succeed often enough that we slowly replaced the old images they had of themselves with brand-new ones.

Step 6: Summary Feedback

If the student brought his summary to the second timing, the tutor went over it immediately, after finishing the congratulatory smiles, of course.

We used four main guidelines for writing summaries. We often printed these guidelines at the top of the back side of each article so the students could see them when writing their summaries. The guidelines were as follows:

- First, write a topic sentence that tells the most important idea.
- Then add other main ideas or the most important details.
- Words from the text *must be spelled correctly*. Find the word in the text, and spell it correctly.
- The summary must be in your own words. Do not copy sentences from the text.

Crafting a topic sentence that states the main idea of an article is a complex skill. So, also, is the ability to distinguish between important and trivial details, the ability to synthesize a list of ideas into one larger idea, and the ability to paraphrase someone else's thoughts. We found two things to be most helpful in teaching these thinking skills. First, we had tutors write summaries of the articles and discuss them with other tutors during professional development activities. In that way, we ensured that all of our tutors were skilled at summary writing and could better discuss students' summaries with them. Second, we trusted the elephant-eating process.

The students wrote their summaries, received feedback on their writing, and rewrote their summaries in response to that feedback. This process entailed a lot of writing, a lot of conversation and interaction, and a lot of rewriting. At the same time, students were reading thousands of grammatically correct sentences and hundreds of thousands of correctly spelled words in the articles, internalizing both, thus making writing easier because they were drawing from a pool of greater language proficiency.

Many teachers told us that the students who had gone through Rewire wrote the best summaries in their subject area classes. The students who were formerly the poorest at writing summaries could now compete with the brightest students on a complex thinking/reading/writing task.

Step 7: Charting

When the students went back to their desks after the second timing, they pulled their progress chart from the left side of their folder. They filled in that day's date and article number and used two different-colored highlighters or markers to record the first timing and the second timing. As shown in figure 5.5 (page 110), the chart is a bar graph, with the second timing score resting on top of the first timing score. This graphic evidence of their improvement reinforced the pride they took in their efforts.

Teachers could also use the chart to analyze whether students were encountering problems and to determine what changes students might need to make in their approach to the work.

Step 8: Finish/Revise Summary

Finally, with any time remaining during Rewire Reading, the tutor tried to check on at least some of the students' revisions on their summaries. The tutor wasn't always able to get to every student every time, but as long as she was able to check some students every day, they took the task of revising their summaries seriously and did the work.

Avoiding Program Problems

Rewire Reading is deceptively simple. Will has encountered many less-than-optimal implementations as he has worked in classrooms. What is critical and what many people miss in reading the schedule and the step-by-step descriptions is the smile. A business-like attitude pervades a Rewire classroom, but it is not a mechanistic one. There exists a human element of, dare I say it, warmth. It is not necessarily the mushy, gushy kind of warmth, and it is definitely not the "I love you so much that I'll bend over backward to accommodate your bad behavior so you can walk all over me" kind.

Students' emotional antennas are finely tuned to rejection and dislike. The tutor may not say a negative word, but if she has a negative attitude toward her students, they pick up on it. If she goes quickly through the schedule, keeping things humming along, but doesn't take that tiny moment to give a genuine smile or a positive comment, she will lose a key opportunity. At what other time during the school day will these students have the opportunity to interact positively one-on-one with an adult? We have the advantage of catching students doing something well, instead of doing something wrong. Over time, this

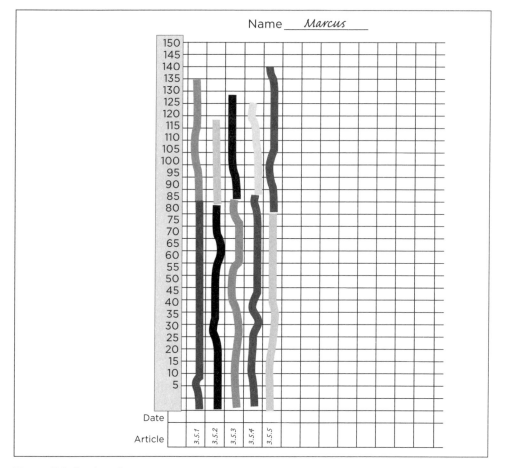

Figure 5.5: Rewire chart.

combination of doing something well and interacting with a tutor who is excited about their improvement can develop the kind of turnaround relationship that each of these students needs.

All it takes is one caring adult for at-risk students to start to care about themselves. So if you have a tutor who is not developing better relationships with her students over time, it is best to catch her early and have her watch a tutor who does this well. If you find that she lacks the ability to change her attitude toward the students, you need to reassign her.

Try to Help Students Who Do Not Want Help

Another common problem with implementing this program is trying to serve students who are not ready for Rewire. Despite our best efforts, some students continued to act out and not comply with the standards of engagement we set for them. If we had allowed them to remain in Rewire, their inertia would have dragged all the other students in their group—and possibly in other groups—down with them.

Our approach at this juncture was critical. We did not punish students for not being ready. We simply met with them and said something like "I like having you in this class, but I just don't think you're ready for Rewire at this point. It's so important to us that you do this right that we're going to drop you from the class. We'll check with you again at the end of the grading period. If you think you're ready at that point and want to give it another try then, we'll give it a go."

Despite their howls of protest and pleading for another chance, we held firm and told students we would give them another chance later. More often than not, we found a changed attitude come next semester, because the students really did value the improvements they were making and their personal contact with the tutor. This, of course, necessitated planning some alternatives with the administration, but it was time well spent in order to ensure that the most disruptive students didn't sabotage themselves and take down others in the process.

Treat Rewire Like a Magic Program

Remember Allington's (2002) conclusion: "programs don't teach, teachers do." We designed Rewire to start getting immediate results, while the tutors were learning how to better teach individual students. Rewire is really a staff-development program that helps teachers and paraeducators be better instructors. If the tutors remember this purpose and stay focused on what they are learning about teaching reading, instead of simply going through the repetitive motions of doing the steps of a program, they will improve and so will their students.

Keep the Principal in the Dark

This last problem touches on a larger issue that affects Rewire interventions: administrative support. In schools where administrators do not fully understand the criticality of need or understand how Rewire is designed to meet that need, dozens of decision points can cause an optimal program to veer off into ineffectiveness. It might be that the science teacher is taking a field trip and wants the paraeducators to serve as chaperones. It might be that a paraeducator is supervising lunch duty and cannot be released five minutes early to head to the Rewire classroom to prep materials and be ready to start students working the instant they walk through the classroom door. It might be that a history teacher wants a bilingual paraeducator in his class every day for the whole period in order to translate for a student, instead of adjusting his instruction and having the paraeducator come to the class after finishing her Rewire duties. It might be assigning thirty students to a classroom without adequate space or tutors, or maybe not releasing tutors for training. Whatever the issue, careful planning can ensure a good implementation, whereas a lack of understanding can ensure that the program fails.

Summary

If we had followed the core leadership principles described in chapter 2 and set up the student–home–educator team communication triangle explained in chapter 3 but had not done Rewire Reading, we would not have achieved the success we did in turning around our students' learning. Our students needed practical help to master what had eluded them for so long. If we had not provided that help in the most practical, intensive, and systematic way possible, all our other efforts would have been greatly compromised, and we would not have gotten the job done. In the same way, just intervening to help build our students' reading, writing, and thinking skills would not have led to our ultimate success by itself. The interventions depended on the other two components of leadership and communication to ensure that the maximum number of students possible kept walking the long, hard, groundbreaking road that revolutionized their learning and opened up a new world of possibilities.

For more information about Rewire Reading, visit www.rewirereading.com.

Chapter 6

OTHER INTERVENTIONS

The previous chapter explained Rewire Reading in detail because it was our most important literacy intervention. Beyond that, it was one of our most critical interventions, period, breaking the failure cycle by turning around the negative beliefs, attitudes, and habits our students had developed and giving them real skills they could use to create success in a job or postsecondary education. But Rewire was not our only intervention. This chapter details some of the other programs and processes we implemented, interventions you can use to turn around your own school.

English Curriculum

We had to make a clear break from tradition when it came to our English curriculum. In one freshman English class I visited, eighteen of twenty-one students were failing (as discussed in chapter 5), and this class was a pretty good reflection of all of our English classes. The students' reading, writing, and thinking skills were so far below grade level that we had to make a choice. Reducing the demands of our curriculum was not an option because we wanted students to graduate with skills, not simply graduate. We could either change our teaching methods, covering the same concepts but using activities that took into account where our students were in terms of their skills, or change our curriculum to focus directly on building their skills. We chose the latter as a more direct route to our goals.

Rationale

Three beliefs helped us decide to change our English curriculum into one that focused on literacy skill development:

1. It is hard to change teaching styles all at once. Differentiating instruction to account for on-level and below-level students is a complex skill that takes time to master, and students would continue to struggle for some time if we focused on instruction.

2. Literacy skills were needed in all other classes, too. This meant that all teachers would have to make the same shift as the English teachers

and do it at the same time. Again, although we knew this was a step our teachers would have to take eventually, we wanted to improve our students' literacy quickly so they could start benefiting from instruction sooner.

3. We had an intervention that would work.

We found that our English staff was willing to restructure in order to better meet our students' need for reading intervention. Based on our early pilot with Rewire Reading, they were fairly certain we could make a huge difference in our students' skills by taking this step.

Classification of Reading Levels

We decided to divide our English classes by reading levels in order to meet students at their current level of need and to create a progression that would keep them continuously growing until they reached grade level. Some of our students were new immigrants and had such low reading skills that reading tests could not accurately measure their level because of their lack of English skills. We considered these students to be at a first-grade level. Other fairly recent arrivals and students classified as learning disabled were scattered from second-grade to third-grade levels. And at the fourth-grade level, we had a larger number of kids who appeared to be remnants of the phenomenon known as the "fourth-grade slump": when books started to contain fewer pictures, more text, and more vocabulary words—typically around the start of fourth grade—these readers stopped reading because they no longer found reading easy, and they fossilized at just about that level of reading.

Students below a fifth-grade level needed a particular focus on making reading easier and building their vocabularies. Students who read from a fifth-grade to an eighth-grade level needed higher-level vocabulary and assistance in thinking through longer, more complex sentences. So we decided to structure our English program according to reading level:

- English 1: Reading levels 1.0–4.9, for students at any grade
- English 2: Reading levels 5.0–7.9, for students at any grade
- English 3: Reading levels 8.0 or higher, freshmen and sophomores
- English 11 and 12: On-level juniors and seniors

In our plan, English 11 and 12 remained as they always had: required courses that all juniors and seniors took. English 1, 2, and 3 were the new courses that took the place of English 9 and 10. If you were at grade level in reading, you took English 3 as a freshman and a sophomore. If you were below grade level, you took English 1 or 2. In both English 1 and 2, we used Rewire Reading as a core strategy, adding writing and traditional literature study in developmentally appropriate ways. We told students in English 1 and 2 that we expected them to make a minimum of two years' growth in their reading level each year so they could move up to a higher-level English class. Following is a more detailed look at our new English courses.

English 3

If you were a freshman or sophomore and your reading level was above an 8.0 as measured by the Gates-MacGinitie test, you would take English 3. English 3 was a two-year course with a looping curriculum. The first year, the class followed the traditional freshman English curriculum, and the next year, it used the sophomore curriculum. So if you entered our high school reading at grade level, you would take English 3 for two years, at the end of which you would have earned two English credits and covered all the material traditionally covered in freshman and sophomore English. This meant that every other year, freshmen studied sophomore literature before they studied freshman literature. We didn't see any problem in breaking up the usual order of things. The usual sequence was an arbitrary construct; freshman literature was not a prerequisite for understanding sophomore literature.

The only problem we could see was when students who took English 2 as freshmen improved their reading skills and moved up to English 3 as sophomores. Wouldn't they have missed the literature experiences that their English 3 classmates had? Moving up was a common occurrence; it was what we expected students to do, so we planned for it. Our English department chose the most significant novels, poems, and short stories that they wanted our English 2 students to read. So if English 3 was comparing *Animal Farm* (Orwell, 1954) with the movie *Stalin* (Duvall, Ormond, Passer, & HBO Pictures, 1993) one year, English 2 also read the book and watched the movie. The way in which the book was read in English 2 accounted for the students' needs—read-alouds, more building of background knowledge and vocabulary focus, breaking the material into smaller chunks and covering it over a longer period of time—but the students had the same seminal experiences as their English 3 counterparts. They had not read all the same literature, but they had read what our English department considered the most important. And the students in English 2 read it well, understanding it with more depth than would have been possible had they read it at a faster pace with their on-level peers.

Objections to English 1 and English 2

Students with low literacy skills were eligible (which is a nice way of saying "required") to take English 1 or 2, depending on their need. The class substituted for their regular English class and counted for English credit.

We had to get approval by the school board for these classes, of course, and we were aware that what we were doing might be controversial. Some raised the objection that we were tracking students. Others said that the work was remedial and not rigorous enough to count as credible, or creditable, high school–level work.

Tracking

The following were our responses to the tracking concern:

1. Students were able to move from one "track," or level, to another. In fact, our students knew that we *expected* them to move up. No one was stuck in a "dummies'" track.

2. Intensive literacy instruction was the demonstrable need of these students, and differentiated instruction within a regular English class, in our opinion, would either not be intensive enough for these students because of the need to teach to all students or would interfere with the learning of the on-level readers.

3. Based on Rewire research, we predicted students would be able to increase two grade levels per year on average. (After we implemented the program, that proved to be the case. As the years went by, we saw a reduction in the need for, first, English 1 classes and, later, English 2 classes. Fewer students needed help because they had improved through our classes.)

Credit

The following were our responses to the credit concern:

1. We were focused on the same Essential Academic Learning Requirements (the Washington State learning goals) in these leveled courses as in our regular English courses. We focused on reading, writing, speaking, and thinking skills in all our English courses.

2. Although students were not reading all the same literature as the on-level courses, we covered the highest-priority literature, using a depth rather than breadth approach. This method ensured rigor and is in alignment with current trends, which are moving away from simply covering the curriculum and moving toward deeper analysis of fewer topics.

3. It was possible to get a passing grade and thus a credit in English 1 or 2 (because students had done everything we had asked them to) and yet not be ready to move up to the next level because their reading had not improved enough. If, after a year, students were not ready to move up, they could retake the class, but they would receive elective credit

only, not English credit. They still had to earn four English credits to graduate, and they still had to take junior and senior English. If that meant doubling up English classes, that was the reality of what the students had to do, but this rule kept our standards high while still allowing us to do everything we could to support their learning.

We knew we were on solid ground when it came to defending our English program because it was preparing the students for upper-level and college-level English coursework while taking into consideration their starting points. We based our decision on what was good for our students, and we were confident that we were offering systemic help: standards-based instruction, scaffolded for the needs of our students to allow them to be successful.

Hard Choices and Sacrifices

We had to make some sacrifices to implement our new English plan. We needed to limit English 1 and 2 to twenty students per class, down from the typical twenty-five to thirty. This meant we needed an extra English teacher. I had to move a former English teacher who had become a migrant student advocate back into the classroom. In addition, I had to cut electives in drama, journalism, and photography, which was hard for everyone, but it was a necessary step.

Another sacrifice that our staff had to make was having less access to paraeducators. Our teachers had come to depend on the bilingual, migrant, and Title I personnel, who could work with students one-on-one in mainstream classrooms to help them achieve more success. In order to have the personnel to do Rewire Reading, we needed to have the paraeducators working in our English 1 and 2 classrooms full time. We explained the options to our staff, and because of the success they saw in our pilot program, they were willing to give up their paraeducators. The teachers saw that we would be helping their students develop the skills to function independently.

This willingness to sacrifice for the common good said much about our teachers, as well as much about how we implemented our leadership principles. We allowed the staff to be a part of collaborative decisions while at the same time influencing their thinking by pointing out how the changes we wanted were both in their own self-interest and what was best for the students.

Comprehensive Literacy Program

We followed a three-pronged method of attack to develop our students' literacy (see fig. 6.1 on page 118). The first prong (Intervention) included interventions we specifically designed for those students who were reading two or more years below grade level. The other two prongs were frequent, self-selected reading (Read-a-Lot) and content-area reading (InfoText) for all of our students.

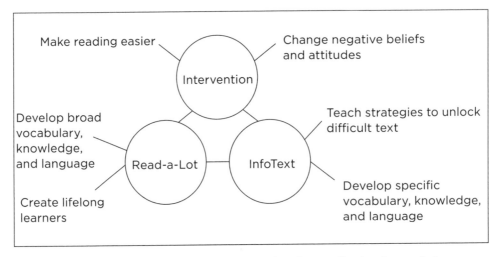

Figure 6.1: Three-pronged literacy plan: a comprehensive reading involvement plan.

Prong 1: Intervention

Although we completely believed in the efficacy of Rewire Reading, we did not want to miss other opportunities for students to improve. We had grant money available to purchase computer software and, after careful deliberation, decided on a Tier 3 intervention program. We were already conducting response to intervention (RTI) Tier 2 interventions, working in small groups, but this program included a more intensive, one-on-one learning opportunity. Its approach was the exact opposite of Rewire. Whereas Rewire was a meaning-focused approach that used decoding approaches only when the tutor deemed it necessary and only at the moment of need, the computer program focused on phonemic awareness and phonics. Its goal was to make the recognition of words automatic so that reading would be easier and comprehension thus improved.

We implemented the software in our English 1 and 2 classes, explaining the theory behind the program. Then we either invited or required students to use the program for twenty to thirty minutes each day in class. The students who were required to use the program were few in number, and we selected them based on their spelling skills; whether they had been making adequate progress with Rewire; whether they were engaging in free, voluntary reading; and the speed at which they seemed to process information. All of these variables were judgment calls, but the last criterion in particular depended on the teacher's perceptions of the student's rate of speech and the think time the student typically needed to respond when asked a question or when participating in a conversation.

This computer program did not work well for our students. The reason could have been the teachers, who were not convinced that the approach would be successful or that it would lead to an increase in free, voluntary reading; they may have transmitted their doubts to students unconsciously. Or it could have been that our students had grown too used to the social interaction of our other reading methods and did not want to be stuck at a computer by themselves. Thus, they would give up when the going got tough—and the going did get tough, because the program was trying to build new neural networks, which took an enormous amount of attention and repetition. We found it hard to keep the students engaged. We decided to stick with our Rewire Reading intervention.

Prong 2: Read-a-Lot

It is not enough to make reading easier for students who are struggling. They need to actually read a lot in order to develop more vocabulary and conceptual knowledge. Malcolm Gladwell (2008), in his book *Outliers*, makes a convincing case for the 10,000 Hour Rule: world-class proficiency in a skill or area of knowledge takes about 10,000 hours of practice or time spent fooling around and experimenting. He cites Bill Gates experimenting with early computers from the age of thirteen, the Beatles playing nonstop gigs in Hamburg, Germany, before they hit it big, and other examples to make the point that aptitude may not be as important as magnitude when it comes to getting good at something. The more time you spend, the better you get.

Read-a-Lot, which was our low-tech name for extensive reading, was the second prong of our literacy program. We continually reminded our students that "smart is not something you are; smart is something you become," and "the more you read, the smarter you get." We also told stories of people who overcame their poverty by making the decision to read a lot. As Mark Twain said, "The man who does not read good books has no advantage over the man who can't read them."

Stocking the Library

If we wanted students to read, we had to give them access to appealing reading materials. To provide such access meant stocking our library so that whatever students' current reading levels were, they could find books to match. We allocated a lot of our budget to stocking our library. Every time the district ran a supplemental budget levy, I put in a request for more books and communicated to the community the importance of having a robust library. The voters always approved the requests, which let us continually build our library.

In order to make it easier for students to find books that matched their reading levels, we considered two programs available at that time: Accelerated Reading (AR) from Renaissance Learning and the Lexile Framework for Reading from MetaMetrics. Both of these programs rated the difficulty of a book not on its content, but on the language difficulty—on the difficulty of the vocabulary and the complexity of the sentences. We could post the resulting rating, a grade level such as 4.5 in AR or a Lexile number such as 700, on the spine of the book so students could see at a glance how hard they would have to work at reading that book.

We reminded students that if they were really interested in a subject or had a lot of prior experience with it, then they would have the motivation—and in the case of prior experience, the prior knowledge—that would enable them to read far above the grade level listed on the spine. In fact, reading above their grade level was something we wanted students to do sometimes to make faster reading gains.

We also scoured the Internet and consulted sources to find recommended book lists of titles that were popular with struggling high school readers. After all, filling a high school library with copies of *Horton Hears a Who!* (Seuss, 1954) and *Where the Wild Things Are* (Sendak, 1963) is inappropriate—unless your goal is to have your students think you are insulting them. Our librarian and Will looked for companies that specialized in high/low books (high interest/low reading level) and read book reviews instead of blindly buying just the books recommended by AR. We knew that many of our students—not addicted to the pleasure of reading but curious about certain topics or people—preferred nonfiction to young adult novels, so it was important to find these kinds of books. We even purchased graphic novels—not the explicit, morality-bending kind, but the modern-day, comic-book kind—for our readers who were the least interested in reading. Such novels were a stretch for our librarian, but we convinced her that they met the needs for some of our students who were not yet hooked on reading and for whom graphic novels were a small step to get them into reading-like behavior.

Creating Classroom Libraries

One of the keys to turning students into willing, enthusiastic readers who read for their own purposes is to give them ready access to a lot of materials. Because we did SSR in advisory, I set aside a small amount of money for teachers who wanted to add magazines or books to their classroom libraries. Students could peruse the library materials after they finished their work in class or choose something new to read in advisory if they no longer had interest in what they were reading. We also encouraged advisors to share or trade materials with other advisors. When Will was receiving a bulk subscription to the newspaper, his room became a popular place for teachers to stop by and pick up a couple copies just before advisory class.

Although we frequently encouraged free reading, we never made an official policy to *require* students to read something of their own choosing when they finished an assignment in class. In hindsight, such a policy is probably one we should have considered strongly. It would not only have fit with the concept of bell-to-bell learning, but also would have helped greatly in developing the reading habit for our students and contributing to their eventually reaching the 10,000-hour plateau required to become a world-class reader. Every long journey is comprised of thousands of small steps, so five minutes to read here and ten minutes there are significant contributions toward arriving at the destination.

Prong 3: InfoText

InfoText, which was our name for content-area reading and the strategies used to read informational text, was the third prong in our comprehensive reading program. Learning to read is one thing; reading to learn is another. We used our staff-development time to examine content-area reading strategies so that teachers could give their students tools and processes to use while reading. That way, students would learn the content and also develop experience with pulling the knowledge they needed out of texts, making them more self-sufficient learners over time.

Will taught our staff various strategies that he took from his experience as a language acquisition specialist and from books such as *Teaching Reading in the Content Areas: If Not Me, Then Who?* by Rachel Billmeyer and Mary Lee Barton (1998). The staff learned a strategy and then tried it on a text during the weekly staff-development time. Then they went back to their classrooms to try the strategy on some lessons that week. At staff-development time the following week, we discussed successes and failures, and teachers determined whether they wanted to keep using that strategy, try it once more to tweak it, or try something different.

As we gained competency in using reading strategies in our classrooms and grew more committed to using them, we started to focus on writing across the curriculum. Writing is the other half of the reading coin. The act of writing improves reading. In the case of writing across the curriculum, reading improves because students are doing expository writing, and by paying attention to the details of organization, elaboration, phrasing, and word choice, students become more aware of these details in the texts they must read.

To develop our skills, we brought in specialists from the state department of education and the local ESD to teach the staff how to score writing. Then we followed up with our in-house experts, who helped our staff create writing assignments that fit their content and develop the rubrics they would use to score them. After an assignment was given in class, we sometimes used our staff-development time to score the students' papers using the rubrics created for the assignment. In this way, we supported our staff in creating quality writing assignments that improved learning, while at the same time helping them learn how to score papers and explain the scoring to their students.

Once we showed our teachers how to score papers, we also trained them how to teach students to score papers. We started the process in the English department by using in-class time to have students work in small groups to score papers. Thus, when teachers in science or history or art wanted to do a writing assignment and have students score them, we had already laid the groundwork and the students already knew the process.

Thinking Maps

Another successful intervention was the use of Thinking Maps™. This particular set of graphic organizers, trademarked by Thinking Maps, Inc., helped us to make our instruction more visual. We used these visual tools with our students as a scaffolding device, a way to support them as they worked at a higher level.

Overcoming the Language of Poverty

Our students needed help in their academic classes because their language skills were lacking. Many of the students spoke what might be called a *language of poverty*. Their language was not unlike that of English learners (ELs) who were learning English as a second language. They had what Jim Cummins (1979) of the University of Toronto describes as BICS, but not CALP.

BICS, or basic interpersonal communication skills, is the language of the home, the street, and the lunchroom. BICS is all the stuff we talk about with parents and friends when we use lots of body language (such as gestures or facial expressions) and changes in our voices (such as pitch, emphasis, volume, or pacing) to give our language more context for understanding. BICS also uses back-and-forth interaction among people to help them communicate their experiences, clarify what they need or want, and find out things they need to know.

CALP, or cognitive academic language proficiency, is the language of the classroom, the laboratory, and the think tank. CALP focuses on ideas and has specialized vocabulary and ways of speaking that are not typically heard in the lunchroom. We experience this kind of language when we read a challenging article on a topic with which we are unfamiliar. CALP provides fewer contextual clues than BICS; it is more abstract, and it is usually not made easier to understand through gestures, facial expressions, or tone of voice like social, interactive talk is. CALP is also more challenging cognitively. The ideas are not as familiar as the ones we encounter in our daily experiences; indeed, they are sometimes so new to us that they feel like a foreign language.

Our students had no trouble expressing themselves socially or understanding basic school talk like simple instructions. What they struggled with was the language of history, science, and math: academic language.

We were afraid that many of our students would *never* develop fluency in the language of academics because they had stopped listening to it long ago. Children grow up learning their native language by paying attention to it and interacting with it, trying to clarify confusion and misunderstanding through trial and error and more observation. A natural human reaction is to clarify confusion, but if something gets too confusing, we might just stop listening, and the information remains incomprehensible.

This is what happens to our students who have impoverished language skills. When academic language gets too confusing, they listen with diminished attention or stop listening altogether, which eventually becomes a habit. If students are not engaged with making sense of the academic language they are hearing, they will not learn the academic language. We might as well be speaking Swahili. Students who have well-educated parents at home or students who read a lot, especially in the area of nonfiction, might have more exposure to this higher-level, academic language and interact with it enough that they learn school talk. But our impoverished students who do not have those advantages will not learn a language they have not heard.

Implementing Thinking Maps

Visual tools, such as graphic organizers and Thinking Maps, make complex language easier to process. They reduce the number of words used to explain a concept down to the key words only, and they show the relationships among those words. These visual tools make the words and ideas stand still so they are easier to think about; the words don't just go tumbling by in a torrent of lecture. Teachers can get students to interact with the ideas by asking them to copy down words and manipulate them into graphic organizers. Students can be asked to explain graphic organizers to a partner or use them to write a summary of concepts. In short, these visual tools make the ideas, and the academic language used to describe the ideas, more understandable; they keep the students engaged in attending to the language; and they make it easier to clarify whatever the student does not understand.

Thinking Maps (www.thinkingmaps.com), with its emphasis on a common set of eight maps and a well-articulated training program, had an advantage over other graphic organizers, and the staff voted to make Thinking Maps our next focus area. I solicited a group of volunteers from different content areas to go through the training and then provide training to the rest of the teachers. This way, we would have experts on staff who were committed to implementing Thinking Maps in their own classrooms and helping others to do the same. Once these teacher leaders had implemented a new Thinking Map in their classes, they could then present what they had done in their classrooms and help the other teachers plan lessons to use the maps.

The Thinking Maps helped our students understand complex concepts. The Thinking Maps also made a very real contribution to improving writing. Students were internalizing the specialized vocabulary and language patterns of the content they were studying, and they could then draw upon that language to write with greater proficiency. Thinking Maps were also a great tool for organizing concepts in an easy-to-follow outline, and academic writing is simply well-organized thoughts written on paper.

Extended Learning Time

There is an old saying that all students are gifted, but some just haven't had enough time to open their packages yet. Some of our students just needed more time to learn what they hadn't learned yet. Many special academies and charter schools share common philosophies about hard work that are expressed in mottos such as "Work hard, be nice," "Work hard, change history," or "We work hard today to make dreams come true tomorrow." We essentially agreed with all of these maxims, telling our students that learning is not always easy, but if you work at it bit by bit and work on it long enough, you will eventually get it. As Albert Einstein said, "It's not that I'm so smart, it's just that I stay with problems longer."

Our district did not have the money, or the cultural capital with our community, to extend our school year or offer Saturday academies, things that would have put us more in line with some of the top-performing schools. But one of our mottos was "Do everything you can with whatever you have," so we looked for other ways to extend our learning time.

We applied for and received grants that allowed us to open our doors both before and after school for students to do extra studying. We had an English teacher who was available in her classroom to help students from 6:20 a.m. until classes began. After school, we had a math teacher available in his classroom, and we opened the library for studying. The teachers who staffed these extended-day sessions were paid a good hourly wage, so finding recruits was not too hard.

What was a little harder was finding students for these teachers to teach. After all, extra hours of study are not what struggling students dream of every night when they fall asleep exhausted from a day of bell-to-bell learning. But at Granger, our philosophy was: it's not enough to offer opportunities for our students to succeed; we have to develop mechanisms that ensure that they do.

Mechanism: The Time-Owed System

The time-owed system was a mechanism that I developed when I was an assistant principal at my previous school, Grandview High School, to attack a huge problem: unexcused absences. As I looked at how to improve learning for our students there, I noticed that we had more than four thousand hours of unexcused student absences in the previous year. That was four thousand hours when students were not in class, and if they were not in class, how could they improve their learning? We had a policy for unexcused absences in our student handbook, which specified progressive discipline in the event that students did not bring in excuses, but with eight hundred students and only two administrators, we had gotten behind in enforcing the policy.

I thought it would be smart to deal with the worst offenders by bringing them all together so I could lay down the law to everyone at once. I asked our attendance secretary to generate a list of the top fifty offenders and write referrals directing them to come to a meeting in our commons area. As the students arrived, I handed each of them a personally addressed discipline referral and went on to explain the contents. I was putting them on notice that this was step one of the progressive discipline process. They were to share the discipline referral with their parents, which was step two of our progressive discipline policy. Now that we had done the first two steps, there was no margin for error. If a student had even one more unexcused absence, we would move him or her to step three: suspension.

I thought this approach was a smart one. What I realized soon after the meeting was that I had opened Pandora's box. My time was consumed with tracking whether these fifty kids were showing up for all their classes, calling truants into my office, having arguments over whether excuse notes had been turned in, and calling in parents for combative suspension meetings. Tracking these students was quickly becoming a full-time job. There had to be a better way.

We needed a mechanism to improve attendance, an emergency stop in the system that would kick in when things were going wrong and correct the problem—and it had to work without hiring a dean of students to run it. The answer came from an unexpected source: Al Capone.

While I contemplated how to solve the problem, I remembered that infamous Chicago mobster. In educational jargon, Capone was gifted and talented. By the age of twenty-six, he already ran Chicago's mob, and by age thirty-one, he rose to the top of his class as public enemy number one. His method of control was intimidation and murder. In the year before he took over as Chicago's mob boss, there were sixteen mob murders. After he took over, the total soon went up to sixty-four murders in a year. Yet the police could not pin anything on him and could not prevent him from committing crimes.

Our attendance policy at school seemed equally as futile in preventing our students from committing absences. We could not fail a student solely due to poor attendance because board policy didn't allow it. As long as students turned in makeup work, which could be accomplished by copying another student's work, they could scrape by with a C or D, and we could not fail them. Many students were just fine with scraping along the bottom, but we were sending them out into the world with substandard skills. Their poor attendance would wreak mayhem on their future in the same way Capone brought pain to a whole city.

But Capone's demise held the solution to our problem. The law finally caught up to him by using the numbers. Capone was making millions through illegal activities, and the Federal Bureau of Investigation (FBI) figured out how to track that. The FBI still could not prove how Capone had gotten the money; they simply knew he had it. Then it dawned on someone that Capone had not paid taxes on any of that money. From that point, it was a simple matter of taking Capone to trial for tax evasion, which they convicted him of easily.

Whereas Capone had stolen tax money from the government, our students had stolen time by being absent from class, time that should have been used to improve their skills and prepare for their futures. Our data-management system provided us with the evidence. Now we just needed to connect that evidence to a simple rule that would make the penalty for the crime swift, unavoidable, and easy to enforce.

Somewhere around that time, I heard about a school that had implemented a time-owed system. For every hour of class that a student missed due to an unexcused absence, the student needed to make up one hour in study hall before or after school.

Hooray! This was the simple rule I was looking for. It was time for our students to repay the debt to their education. Over the next year at Grandview High School, we cut unexcused absences by 50 percent.

Granger High School had the same problem when I arrived. In my first year, our much smaller student body racked up nearly two thousand hours of unexcused absences. Based on what I had learned at Grandview, we set about implementing a system to combat the problem, but with a few new twists. What follows is how we crafted the unexcused absences portion of our new attendance policy:

1. Every hour of unexcused time will result in one hour of study session.

2. Grade/credit will not be given for any class in which time is owed.

3. When time is owed, students cannot participate in any extracurricular sports or activities unless a student's grade is directly affected.

Note that in point 1, we assign a study session instead of detention. If we truly wanted kids to make up for lost learning time, then we needed to have them study or develop their reading skills by reading self-selected materials. Picking up garbage on campus or other such activities may have served as deterrents, but not as motivators. In my mind, the goal in discipline is to somehow gear it toward academic and skill set development rather than being punitive. Why should students get suspended from school for skipping school? That practice does not make sense (at least in most cases). Our kids may not have seen forced attendance at study sessions as a privilege, but they understood the rationale, and they knew they could control whether they had to attend before or after school by showing up for work during regular school hours. Because we had a lot of unexcused absences in the beginning, we effectively solved our problem of getting students to take advantage of our extended-day tutoring programs. Yes, the time was nonvoluntary, but it exposed students to the resources available and let them know they could get real help when they needed it. After experiencing study hall a time or two, they were more likely to go back on a voluntary basis when needed.

We developed point 2 because it did not violate the board's policy about not being able to give an F due to poor attendance. The difference is subtle but went unchallenged by students and parents. We were not giving students an F; we were giving them an incomplete until they completed the requirements of the course. We would hold the grade indefinitely until all time was made up. This change was the firm line that some of our foot-draggers had to be held to before they would take us seriously. We kept the parents informed when students were not making up their time, but if students waited until the end of a grading period and angry parents started demanding grades, we could point to our policy. The board had approved it; we had informed the students and parents of the policy and the rationale for it; and students had no way out except to make up the hours owed.

Point 3 was the real clincher for many students, because they attended school to play sports or participate in activities like school plays. We had to educate our coaches, especially those who did not also teach at the school, about why we had this policy and help them plan for how to make sure their athletes were attending classes and making up time quickly when they did skip.

Our librarian aide helped us enormously when she volunteered to be the coordinator of our new program. She believed passionately in holding kids accountable for making up their work. By accessing our data-management system in the office, she could transfer a list of all students who had unexcused absences each week into a time-owed spreadsheet. She added new hours to any that students already owed and put lists in the advisors' mailboxes each week that showed who owed what. As students made up their hours, she updated the spreadsheet.

Peer Pressure

Eventually, the coordinator started to print the time-owed sheets on full-sized posters. Every Monday, we hung a new set of these posters in the hall outside the library. Some might call this new way of motivating students "shaming" because there was a pretty good deal of ribbing among the students when one of their friends' names appeared on the wall. We liked to think of it as "transparency." Unwanted behaviors that were once easy to hide no longer seemed quite so cool when they were tracked for everyone to see.

Parental Pressure

In addition to peer pressure, when we implemented our parent communication system, we were able to bring parental pressure to bear as well. At each parent conference, we talked about the importance of attendance and explained our policies. If a student had already accrued some time owed or was in the habit of missing classes, we discussed that. If parents wanted, advisors could write down in the PEP that they would call the parents if the student owed, for example, more than six hours at any one time. This communication effectively prevented the angry end-of-the-year parents from showing up at my office door.

Teachers used the "Do I need to call your parents?" threat to good effect. But if that did not work and students did not show up for a certain period of time to make up hours, we then instructed the teachers in whose classes they had earned the unexcused absences not to let them into class and to send them instead to the office. The problem was immediately escalated to the administrative level so we could apply more pressure or delve more deeply into the situation to see what might be done to correct the situation.

Principal Pressure

The most effective administrative-level pressure we concocted was probably when I showed the students what would happen if they continued on the path they were treading. Just before the end of the first semester, we made a list of all the students who were not making adequate progress toward making up their hours. We gave the list to the teachers along with a note to send the students to our cafeteria immediately after taking roll in first period the next day. When the motley crew assembled, I proceeded to give them their wake-up call. If they were not going to make up their hours and bring up their failing grades, it was obvious to me that their teachers and I had failed to motivate them. The system we had in place was not working for them, so we were going to make a change and put them into a system that might have a better chance of working. If these students did not take action to change their behavior and show us that our current system would work for them, then we would transfer them to the alternative school at the next semester.

Up to that point, the threat may have seemed like the kind of vague, idle threat that kids who are used to getting in trouble have heard a lot in their lives. So I told them to go get their coats because we were going on a field trip to visit their "new school." We walked across the street to the portable classroom that housed the alternative high school. The contrast was stark. The old portables that we inhabited while our current building was being remodeled were well worn. Our new building was clean and bright, and we worked hard with the students from the moment we moved in to respect it and keep it nice.

We spent time with the teacher and her instructional aide talking about the program. The students already in the alternative high school either looked suspiciously at this bunch of potential classmates who posed the threat of invading their turf or pointed and winked and reestablished old connections with the visitors. We showed the prospective students that by opening the adjoining classroom in the portable, we would have room to house all of them. They would go to school in those two classrooms all day, eat lunch only with their alternative school classmates, and be completely isolated from the students at the regular high school. For many, this experience was a real eye-opener. The social life they had developed at the high school was more important than anything else, and they would do anything to hold on to that. For others, the smaller class size and personal attention, or even being able to escape from the social scene and problematic relationships with other students and teachers at the high school were selling points, and they realized they would rather take an alternative route.

Did the tour work? We had a number of students who put in their makeup time. But it didn't work all at once. Some kids didn't make up the time they missed, so we sent them to alternative school. We had to keep our word. Students who went to alternative school knew we meant business, but we also told them that there was a way out. If they did what they needed to at alternative school and got the job done, we would consider them for readmission to the high school after one semester. The door was always open, but to walk through the door, they had to earn it.

So eventually, our tour was highly successful. When we made the promise to transfer kids to the alternative school if they did not make up their hours and bring up their grades, they knew we meant it. For some, that was the motivation they needed. Others found the help they needed in alternative school, where the whole environment was geared to motivating and teaching our neediest kids in an environment where they could get a new start. Some students stayed in the alternative school and graduated from there, but others worked extra hard to get back to where they wanted to be: with all of their friends.

We never got down to zero unexcused absences, but by implementing these procedures, the number of posters on the wall outside the library steadily decreased. By the end of our first year, we had cut the hours of unexcused absences from 1,945 to 741. And most of those 741 were not simply lost hours; they were traded hour for hour. A lost hour of class time was exchanged for another opportunity to learn and build skills for the future, which is all we really wanted anyway.

Mechanism: Nothing Lower Than a C

Shortly after we put the before- and after-school programs in place in the fall of 2001, we implemented another new mechanism. We found another way to encourage students to use our extended-day learning opportunities: we drew a line in the sand (that is, we set strict rules) for our students who were failing two or more classes at the time we held our fall parent conferences, which had been pushed back to December because of construction at our school. The student, his or her parents, and the advisor went over a letter (see the appendix, page 183) that explained to parents that their student's performance was endangering his or her ability to graduate. The letter stated that if the student did not attend extended-day programs and improve his or her grades, "then other alternative educational programs may be more suitable for his or her needs." We listed the alternative high school, GED programs, and Job Corps as options beginning with the second semester, which was five weeks away. We asked the parents to sign the letter to indicate their understanding that it was their responsibility to encourage their child to attend the study sessions and bring up his or her grades. The student and the advisor also signed the letter to indicate that everyone understood what was at stake and what needed to be done.

Although we did have to transfer some of our students into alternative programs, most rose to the challenge. Our taking a stand helped to decrease the number of students who were losing credits, and thus, we cut our dropout rate. We also filled up our extended-day study sessions with students who were working hard to bring up their grades and control their fate.

The line-in-the-sand strategy was a good start, but we needed to move the line closer toward our destination. Scraping by with Ds would not produce the kind of skills, knowledge, or habits that would lead to success after graduation.

In late 2004 or early 2005, I heard of a school that had implemented a policy that students could not have lower than a B in any class. The cutoff to demonstrate proficiency on the state test was 80 percent, so this school reasoned that students needed to perform at that level in class if they were to have a chance to pass the state test. Their new policy told students that if they had anything lower than a B in any class and working in class was not bringing up the grade, then the students had to come in for extra help before or after school.

This concept started me on a little research. I looked at the past few years of our students' grades in English and compared them with their results on our computerized MAP assessment. Then I cross-referenced this data with the scores students received on the WASL test in reading and writing. I discovered that we did not have a single student who was on level on the MAP or who had passed the WASL who was getting a D or F in English. If students wanted to meet our state standards, it seemed unlikely they could do it with a grade of D or F.

I brought my research to a faculty meeting to see how our teachers would feel about implementing a new policy like the one I had read about. The staff liked the idea; they realized that kids who graduated with low skills were not much better off in the long run than those who dropped out. But like me, they thought the standard might be too high a hurdle for our students if we set the bar at a B. We decided to make the policy that Ds and Fs would no longer be acceptable. Any students who did not have an A, B, or C in a class would be referred to extended-day study sessions until they brought their grades up to at least a C. The sooner students brought up their grades, the sooner they could discontinue mandatory attendance at study sessions.

Just as I brought the staff into this decision as a team effort, it was now time to bring in the students so that we were doing education with them, not to them. I realize that some of the mechanisms in this chapter were unilateral decisions. In cases of clear-cut failure—unexcused absences and failing grades—students left us little choice. But this was not a case of clear-cut failure. In the case of Ds, students needed to understand why their grades were no longer good enough, why Ds really were as bad as failure.

We planned an assembly so I could help this decision make sense to students on their terms. Once students were seated, I brought them right back to their feet when I told them I had a special song for them and out blasted the Jackson 5 singing "ABC." We played the whole song and let students (and teachers) get up and dance. Our school culture was one of hard work *and* fun, so this was not an unusual move for us at an assembly. After the song was finished, I used a PowerPoint presentation to explain why "ABC" was the only music that would allow them to dance their way to their dreams. The old-fashioned practice of giving Ds and Fs still described poor performance, but we could no longer in good conscience simply describe poor performance. We wanted something better for our students. We wanted to change poor performance, not just describe it. We showed them the research that linked grades with skill development and test scores, and we reviewed data about how much students had been improving to give them positive affirmation and tell them that we knew they could do this. Students could count on us to support them in getting the job done.

In short, we tried to capture their hearts and imaginations, and then we opened the dialogue. We let students ask questions in the assembly. We told them that this policy would not go into effect until the next semester and that we were open to hearing any suggestions about how to make our idea better. The bottom line was that we did not want students going out into the world without the skills to be successful, and we would work as hard as they did to make sure that did not happen. Similar conversations continued for the next several weeks in advisories and with individual students. Students prone to Ds were not necessarily happy, but they were not openly adversarial. We had successfully moved them up the teamwork continuum.

After the assembly, we sent letters to the parents that explained our new policy. The letter included an attached referral form titled "Academic Success Referral" (see the appendix, page 184; visit **go.solution-tree.com/schoolimprovement** to download the reproducibles in this book). This was the form that teachers would fill out and send home whenever students' grades dropped below a C. The form contained a list of the times and meeting places for all our different extended-day programs and a place for the parent's signature.

Our policy was not an official policy, to be honest. The weight of law was probably not 100 percent behind us, so this policy was not one for which we sought board approval. What we were actually doing was setting up an expectation more than anything else. Just as we did when we told parents that students could not register for next semester's classes if the parents did not attend parent conferences (see chapter 3), we were stating what we wanted for the students, trying to make it sound like compliance was not optional.

Once we put our policy in place, some kids definitely resisted us, but no parents came forward to fight it. They knew we had the best interests of their children in mind. I planned to meet with any parents who challenged the policy privately to discuss their objections. If they remained adamant that Ds and Fs were good enough for their children, I would ask them to sign a form saying so. The form would also state that the parents understood that grades of F would lead to their child falling behind academically and that the result would be eventual placement in a more suitable educational setting.

The end result of our nothing-lower-than-a-C policy was that the number of F grades dropped from 278 to 138 in one semester. The policy did not make students who had to attend our extended-day programs happy at the time, but we held firm while at the same time using the soft relational tools of our mentorship class to keep it from becoming a prison-like environment.

Mechanism: Retake Tests

We designed all of our instructional interventions to engage the students more deeply in their work. We designed our extended learning opportunities to get students to work longer, to make up for time missed in current classes, and to make up for lost time over the years when their bodies were in class but their minds were far, far away. With the implementation of our nothing-lower-than-a-C policy, we were forcing students to come in and spend extra time. But something was wrong with our system.

It was a fight to get many of our students to come in for help, even with the supportive three-way communication we had in place with their families. When students did come in for extended learning opportunities, their motivation often seemed low. They did not seem to be working with a sense of urgency and purpose. We were not getting students to engage more deeply, and if we could not do that, we would lose the battle.

What was getting in the way of students pouring their passion into improving?

I watched how hard the students worked when properly motivated. But because they came to us with such low skills, they had a lot of ground to make up, and despite their hard work, they still often failed the test. And that was where we were losing them. Once they had failed a test, they were stuck with a bad grade—no reward for all their efforts. It was game over, and that was killing their motivation.

When our kids took the statewide WASL test, there was no time limit because it was a criterion-referenced test. We encouraged our students who needed more time to keep working until they felt confident they had done their best. Although our official testing time ended around 11 a.m., we kept one testing classroom open as long as we had students who were still working. Some students would work all day long, forcing us to bring their lunch to them and excuse them from their other classes. They took the test seriously. They cared. The difference was that we were not calling end of game on them before they had set up for their final shot.

Our teachers could not wait to give a test in their classes until every student was ready to take it without the flow of the class grinding to a halt, but what if students had the opportunity to retake any test they had failed? They had demonstrated their willingness to work hard for important things. I knew that if students had another chance, they would keep working, and that was exactly what we wanted.

Now the question became, How could I get the staff to buy into retaking tests? I could mandate a new policy of test retakes, but that would create a lot of extra work for the teachers and a lot of resentment. Their efforts, like those of the discouraged students, would be halfhearted at best.

So I began to bring the idea up at faculty meetings but didn't force any action on it. I simply wanted the staff to think about it. This problem was one we all wanted to solve. How could we get the kids to work longer, read more, and spend more time on the concepts they needed to learn?

I told the staff that as I contemplated the problem, I remembered how I had failed my driving test in high school but I had worked hard to retake it and pass.

My brother took an electrician's test. He knew it was a tough test, and he studied hard to pass it so he could have a good career. He passed it the first time, but even if he hadn't, he knew that he could have retaken the test. You can bet that my brother would have worked twice as hard to pass the test the second time around if he had failed it the first time.

Wasn't that the way all the professions worked? Accounting, nursing, and legal careers: all had professional certification tests, and all of them gave individuals the chance to study longer and retake the test if necessary. If you're motivated and you want something, you keep working until you know you've got it, and then you demonstrate it. Along the way, you become a better student of the subject: a better reader, writer, and thinker; more knowledgeable and more expert.

If my logic was impeccable, my results weren't. The staff balked at first. I just kept bringing the subject up. "This is not going to help prepare them for college," some teachers said. "They don't have continuous retakes in college." I reminded the teachers that the kids we were talking about, the ones with the Ds and Fs, didn't even have the skills to go to college yet. They never would if we didn't do something different. This new policy might allow these students to stay engaged long enough to develop those skills. Then they could not only enroll in college, but they could have the skills needed to pass tests the first time.

The staff agreed to the policy by the end of the year. The big obstacle was that allowing students to retake tests would create more work for teachers, because they would have to create and duplicate more tests. So I dug into the Title I budget that was set up for improving instruction to find the extra money to pay them. We had been using this money for teachers to do other extra work, such as curriculum alignment. With the promise of being fairly compensated for the extra work, and with the undeniable logic of the idea presented for discussion over the course of several months, how could teachers say no? The policy was good for the students; it would ultimately be good for the teachers. The staff agreed that they would let students retake tests as long as they were showing a serious effort to try to learn the material. We presented it to the school board as an addition to our student handbook in order to make it an ongoing, formal part of our system.

I knew the policy was really working when I overheard a conversation while supervising prom. A student approached the science teacher, who was chaperoning. On such a glamorous night, one would expect academics to be the furthest thing from a student's mind, but I clearly remember her saying, "Remember, Mrs. Conroy, I have to retake my science test on Monday." That was the sweetest music I heard that night.

Math Interventions

As bad as our reading and writing scores were when we began our school turn-around, our math scores were even worse. In our baseline year of 2000–2001, when our sophomores had been through nearly two years of my leadership at Granger High School, their reading and writing scores were 20 percent and 11 percent, respectively, meeting standard on our state test. Their math proficiency was 4 percent, compared to the state average of 39 percent (see fig. 6.2).

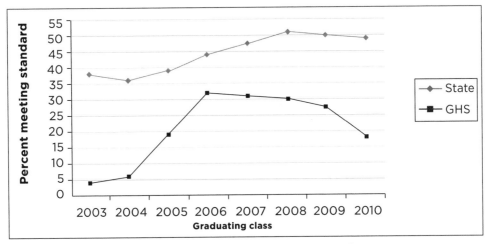

Figure 6.2: Granger WASL math scores compared to Washington State average.

As you can see, the math intervention was our most difficult. We made significant progress in the early years, far outperforming similar populations of Hispanic and low-income students in our state. Still, at our best, we only narrowed the gap between our students and the state average for all students from that initial 35 percent in 2001 to a 13 percent gap in 2004.

As we looked at our data, we had to consider where our students were coming from. Figure 6.3 (page 136) makes it clear that we made huge strides in our students' skills from what they had when they came to us from the elementary and middle schools. After a big jump for the class of 2005 and again for the class of 2006, we hit a plateau where we were still outperforming their earlier scores from elementary and middle schools, but we were not gaining on the state average. Because we were a school with about one hundred students per grade level, we did not consider a change of one or two percentage points to be too descriptive of the quality of our instruction—it was only the difference between one or two students performing better or worse. But trends were important, and while we were not dropping significantly, we were not making the gains we had earlier. The sudden drop-off, especially for the class of 2010, was disconcerting.

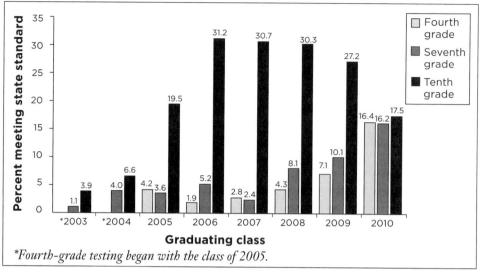

Figure 6.3: Improvement in our students' math scores over the years.

Problem of the Period

To encourage bell-to-bell teaching, we had asked teachers to do entry tasks in all their classes. In the fall of 2002, we simply shifted our emphasis and asked the teachers in our ninety-minute-block classes to start the first ten minutes of class on Mondays with a math problem. We called this entry task "problem of the period." By this time, we had hired an instructional facilitator, and he put together the problems, working with our math staff and consulting with guides from our state. He also solicited entry tasks from the teachers to try to incorporate more problems that would be relevant to different content areas.

Students and teachers worked on these problems for about seven to eight minutes and then used our networked TVs to broadcast a video clip of the instructional facilitator explaining how to solve the problem. We used this video clip because many of our teachers didn't feel confident in explaining how to solve the problems themselves. Eventually, we started to let teachers work on the upcoming problems during our just-in-time staff development, getting help from the math teachers and each other so they gained the skills to solve the problems and explain them to their students. This led to higher student engagement in solving the problems because students realized that their teachers, who were themselves not gifted at math, were working hard to solve the problems, too.

Encouraged by our jump in math scores in 2003 (the class of 2005 in fig. 6.3), we extended our problem of the period an extra day and did these entry tasks on Mondays and Tuesdays the next year. We were rewarded with another big jump in scores that spring.

Why Our Math Interventions Were Not as Successful as We Hoped

The WASL represented a change in what we expected of students in math, and the statewide scores reflected it. Whereas the reading and writing scores topped out in the range of 80–85 percent of students meeting standard in the state, math scores never rose above 51 percent meeting standard in the years I was at Granger. We were not alone in our struggles. However, this was no excuse for not getting closer to the state average. The following sections include the things that caused us problems, which I realized in hindsight.

Curriculum Match

The concepts that were on the state test were not being taught in our classes. In comparison to English, the math curriculum is much more rigid in sequence. Success in more advanced skills is dependent on success with more basic skills, which students learned earlier. We didn't adjust our curriculum enough to compensate for all the knowledge gaps with which students came to us. If we did adjust the curriculum to work on the students' gaps, it left us with inadequate time to cover all the things that were on the test. We tried using a software program in our advisories and extended-day learning programs, but this wasn't enough.

It's also not as easy to integrate math into the curriculum as it is to integrate reading. We asked students to read in almost every class. We gave our teachers the tools to help students learn to be better readers. But we did not find a way to similarly involve math in all classes. In reading, we had our Read-a-Lot program to encourage independent practice. We didn't have anything like that for math.

Level of Expertise

We had lots of expertise in reading; I had recruited Will, an adolescent literacy consultant, to guide and train us on integrating reading and writing. We didn't have such an advantage in math.

If we were to start over, we would have gone to any school that was having a high level of success in math and learn from them. We looked in our state, but we didn't find a mentor school while I was at Granger. Perhaps we should have expanded our search nationally or asked our ESDs and Washington State Department of Education personnel to help us find mentors.

I often asked Will if it was possible to create a math class that was like Rewire Reading, using small groups for discussion, a structure that would move students rapidly with no time to get off task, provide measurable results, and so on. He agreed that such a program would be a good idea, but as a person who did not excel at math, he didn't have the expertise to do it. And because he and all of our teachers were stuck in the dailiness of teaching, we had no time to explore the idea.

Not Held to Standard

As 2008 approached, the year when students were going to be held accountable to pass the math WASL in order to graduate, our state recognized that its schools were in trouble. With only 50 percent of our state's students meeting standard, that meant 50 percent would fail to graduate. Of course, the students would be able to try again as juniors and seniors to pass the test after further study, but this outcome was still a scary prospect. The problem was obviously systemic, rather than a problem with individual students. At that point, the legislature voted to delay the requirement that graduating students must have passed the math portion of the test. Although this was the right decision, it probably partially explains our dip in math scores in 2008. A friend related that at a nearby high school, more than two hundred students attended after-school tutoring to prepare for the math test. After the state requirement was dropped, tutoring-session attendance dropped to just a handful. Holding tough on standards is definitely a key element in keeping students working.

The Key to Success in Any Intervention

Remember, the most critical element in any school improvement initiative is whether it has an impact on the moment-by-moment activities that teachers and students do in the classroom and how deeply the students engage in those activities. Holding workshops and studying instructional manuals are worthless if classroom practice does not change. Never mistake activity for achievement. The only way to ensure that strategies learned are implemented—and implemented well—in the classroom is to dedicate adequate professional learning time that includes time for experimentation before classroom trials, sufficient trial-by-classroom time, and reflection time afterward to examine ways to improve the initial implementations. Just because an initiative does not work the way the manual said it would work does not mean the strategy is flawed. It only means that our use of the strategy is not yet perfect or we have not adapted it well enough to the particular, unique needs of our students. Our motto must be "Analyze, adjust, and try, try again," not "Well, that didn't work."

Chapter 7

TURNAROUND FROM THE INSIDE OUT

This chapter, like previous chapters, is about how we restructured education in order to turn around our students' learning, but in a different way. Instead of explaining how we changed external structures such as our conference system, English curriculum, or student handbook, this chapter focuses on how we restructured the internal worlds of everyone involved with our school. This chapter is about the importance of motivation, beliefs, and attitudes and what we did to make sure all the work we were doing on external factors would not be sabotaged by what was going on in the hearts and minds of the members of our school community.

It is one thing to plan a turnaround, but how do you get people, especially those weighed down by years of negative experience, to buy in to your changes? For me, the answer was fairly obvious. With apologies to Robert Fulghum and his famous essay . . .

(Almost) All I Really Need to Know I Learned in Traffic Safety

As a new teacher, jobs were scarce, so I picked up a certificate to teach traffic safety education in order to be more marketable. In my first job, I ended up teaching consumer math, general math, physical education, and traffic safety. It didn't take me long to notice that some of the notoriously bad students in other classes were very different when it came to traffic safety. When I told my students they had to be at school by 6 a.m. for driving lessons and not one minute later, they arrived by 5:55 a.m. When I assigned homework and told them they had to read it and be prepared by the beginning of the next driving session or they could not drive, they did their homework. Ninety-five percent of my students learned the material successfully and passed the class. In fact, many of the students who struggled in other classes outperformed the National Honor Society students when it came to my traffic-safety class.

Obviously, these students were motivated. They wanted something, and they wanted it badly. Before the first day of class, I filled out the certificates that would serve as their proof to the Washington State Department of Licensing that they had passed their traffic-safety course, typing each student's name onto his or her own certificate. At the first class session, I passed them out, letting the students hold them to experience for just a few moments what this class was all about. At that time, our state law required that to get a driver's license you had to be at least eighteen years old unless you passed a certified traffic-safety course. Sixteen-year-olds who had a traffic safety education certificate in hand were eligible to take their driver's license test. My students were all between fifteen-and-a-half and sixteen. Two years is an awfully long time to wait at that age.

I had their complete attention when I told them to hand back the certificates. "That certificate that you just held in your hands doesn't belong to you yet," I said. "There's nothing I would like more than to hand it back to you in a few months and then hear back from you that you passed your driver's test and you now have your license. But . . ." Here, I paused for dramatic effect. "I drive every day. My wife drives every day. Oftentimes, we have our kids with us. My friends all drive. Bottom line, I cannot put you out there on those roads to endanger me, my family, my friends, and our community. If I'm not convinced that you will be a safe, responsible driver, then instead of handing you your certificate at the end of this course, here is what I'll have to do." At this point, I would hold up one of the certificates with both hands and proceed to tear it, first in half, then in quarters, and again, tearing it smaller and smaller.

The message was clear. My students wanted a driver's license passionately. They knew they had to meet the standards to get it, and they knew they had all the guidelines outlined in the class syllabus. Furthermore, the rationale I gave them for the guidelines made a lot of sense to them, especially when I told them the following truths.

"I'm going to be really tough on you in this class because I don't want you to go through what I went through," I said. "I failed the driver's test twice before I finally passed it. Do you know how humiliating that felt?" Did they know? Of course they did! I had just brought out the number-one fear of these students, that they would fail their test and not get their license while many of their friends gloated that they had passed it. Now their teacher was telling them that he had failed it? Even those students who had felt pretty confident suddenly felt a little less cocky.

I went on to explain how I was a farm kid who had learned to drive at a young age by driving a tractor. My traffic-safety teacher didn't really prepare me for the test. The first time we went out driving, I followed the same basic patterns I used when driving a tractor, and my instructor saw that I could stop, go, and keep the car between the white lines, so he figured I was doing fine; in fact, he told me I was a good driver. At the end of my two—two!—driving sessions, he even had me stop by the local drive-in. He bought two milkshakes, one for him and one for me, and he told me again that I was a good driver. I figured you couldn't get much better than that. But when I got to the written portion of my driver's test, I didn't know the rules, and I failed it. That was embarrassing, but I studied for the written test and was able to pass it the second time I took it. Then came the driving test. I was so embarrassed when I failed it. No one had taught me how to parallel park, how to back around a corner, or what to do at a four-way stop. I had to go back a third time to take the test before I finally passed both portions. So my driving instructor failed me even though he gave me a passing grade for the class.

"I'm going to make sure you are prepared for that driver's test," I told my traffic-safety students. "If I give you back that certificate, you're going to know you earned it, and you're going to be confident that you will pass your driver's test. I refuse to send you out of here unprepared." Although my students would sometimes buck against the rules I set, as any teenager would do, the image of that certificate tearing, the sound of the paper ripping, and my own true story of humiliation stuck with them, and they'd almost always get themselves straightened out in order to avoid their own humiliation.

I had developed a track record of success and could tell the class that 95 percent of my previous students had passed the test. That gave them faith and made them willing to work hard. They believed they would be successful if they did what I asked, because they knew others had been successful. When people are afraid they might fail, a subconscious part often goes to work in their psyche to convince them not to even make an effort. Because my students knew I was committed to them, that I would prepare them so they wouldn't be humiliated like I had been, and because they could see the results of my former students, their belief grew stronger than their fear. We had overcome the debilitating fear of failure that plagues so many and replaced it with a belief in their success. My students were able to put forth their best effort.

The understanding of what truly motivated my traffic-safety students to be so successful would shape my understanding of how to motivate all our students at Granger High School to be successful. I learned that the kids in traffic safety succeeded because of the following:

- They brought with them a strong desire based on what they wanted for their future (motivation, relevance, connection to their reality).

- They knew that I would teach them what they needed to know (trust, relevance).

- They believed they could learn the skills and pass the test (faith in themselves, belief).

The trick would be to apply that specific success more broadly to schooling in general, but before explaining that process, let me tell you two more stories that were critical in shaping how we transformed so many of our students from the inside out.

The Power of Belief and Internal Reality

With that first teaching job came the opportunity to coach the sport I loved: wrestling. After several years of rebuilding the program, I had a very solid team with many experienced wrestlers who were seniors. Eight of the athletes had twenty or more wins that year, and twenty wins is an exceptional number. All of them wrestled well in the season-ending district tournament and advanced to the regional tourney. At regionals, they were again successful, and our team advanced to the Washington State Wrestling Tournament. One newspaper ranked our team tenth in the state, but many coaches from other teams thought we would finish in the top four. I had to agree with them; I thought we were going to finish strong. After all, I had carefully planned our success, making sure we entered tournaments in all four corners of the state earlier in the season. That way, my guys would know they had wrestled against the best competition and would not be intimidated.

When the tournament was over, however, we had not finished in the top four. We hadn't even finished in the top ten. Not one of my wrestlers made it to the finals. They flat out did not compete. What had gone wrong?

I had unknowingly missed a very important factor along the way. My athletes were small-town kids, used to going to other small towns to wrestle other small-town kids. Now we were in one of our state's largest cities, in the bright lights of a huge indoor arena. The whole atmosphere was different from anywhere they had been before. I can see now that my wrestlers weren't sure if they belonged on such a glittery stage. They may not have been aware of it, but their internal self-talk was not a stream of confidence-building thoughts. It was more focused on doubts about the future in this strange new environment than it was on the facts of what they had accomplished in the past. By not addressing this concern and getting my wrestlers to focus on those past successes, I did not adequately prepare their belief system. They did not believe they were going to succeed.

Watching our athletes go from strong and confident one week to weak and hesitant the next perplexed me so much that I decided to focus my master's thesis on sports psychology and the power of beliefs to aid or hinder performance. Through my research, I developed a better understanding of the following:

- Performance is intimately connected to our beliefs about whether we think we can or can't.

- Our beliefs about our capabilities do derive somewhat from our past performance, but it is more accurate to say that our beliefs are connected to what we tell ourselves about our past performance, and we are affected by what others tell us about our performance, too.

This belief–performance link does not just occur in sports. The same dynamic is at play in how students perform in school. My students in traffic safety knew they could pass the driver's test. Because they knew they would be successful if they did what I asked them, they jumped in wholeheartedly. But how did our students at Granger feel about our state WASL test? Many of them were unknowingly looking at it in the same way my wrestlers looked at the state wrestling tournament. They didn't really know if they belonged. They didn't know if they had the skills.

Preparing students for competing against the high standards that had been set for them was important. This preparation included not only having them wrestle daily in our classrooms with the kinds of tasks they would have to perform on those high-stakes tests, but also telling them explicitly what we wanted them to tell themselves: they would be successful if they did the work. My wrestlers needed me to tell them that they had wrestled against the best in the state, that they had been successful, that the mat they were going to walk out on for their matches was no different from any other mat they had wrestled on, and that this was the moment they had been looking forward to and slaved and sacrificed for, so go for it!

We needed to remind the students how prepared they were becoming and tell them that whatever they could do in the walls of our classrooms they could do on the WASL and beyond. We didn't want students to believe, like my wrestlers had, that they were small-town kids who couldn't compete in a bigger world. We had to help them overcome the belief that being born poor or brown or in a small town were handicaps they couldn't overcome. If our students had not yet developed good reading and writing skills, if they had not yet become good in math, we had to help them believe that the operative word was *yet*.

My next story involves a commercial I saw on TV several years ago. I think it was recruiting for one of the branches of the military, and while I no longer remember the words, the images stick with me to this day. The scene was a backyard barbeque at a Latino family gathering. Everyone looked and dressed alike except for one young man who stood out. He was wearing a crisp military uniform, and his parents and relatives looked at him with great pride. He had done something to become different; he was going places, and this brought them great joy. A younger brother, about ten years old, went over and sat down in the serviceman's lap. The older brother looked down at him, took off his military cap, and placed it on the youngster's head. The little boy went incandescent, looking up at his older brother with lights in his eyes. No words were needed to explain that he was thinking, "I want to be just like you." In that moment, that little boy's world expanded from backyard barbeques to possibilities far beyond the walls of his existence.

We worked at Granger to show our students a picture of the possibilities for their futures. Because most of my staff hadn't grown up in the same circumstances as our impoverished or chronically struggling students, they needed ways of communicating with the students that would build a bridge between the students' current reality and the possibilities we wanted them to believe in. What we needed in order to help students create a new reality were strategies, images, and language that were as powerful as what I saw in that commercial. We wanted students to believe in the future of limitless possibility that could be theirs if they would work hard and develop 21st century skills.

The rest of this chapter details the strategies we used:

- To motivate students
- To change the negative beliefs students had about themselves
- To help students to see and believe in a better future
- To help change the negative beliefs of our whole community so that they did not sabotage our students' fledgling efforts to change

Motivating Students

In 1999, a friend from another high school sent me an article from her school newspaper showing that a high school graduate would earn $420,000 more over his lifetime than a high school dropout (Everett Area High School, 1999). Before we talked about this fact in advisories, I wanted to craft a visual message that would motivate all our staff and students. While I was still pondering how to do this, I happened to watch *Happy Gilmore* (Simonds & Dugan, 1996), a movie in which comedian Adam Sandler plays a former hockey player who, improbably, becomes a championship golfer. And suddenly, there it was: the huge, oversized check they presented to him as the winner of the golf tournament. Perfect! Now I had a visual item—the check—that could help my students envision a new reality.

For our next assembly, I had a check printed on posterboard, two feet tall by four feet wide. The check read, "Pay to the order of high school graduate. Amount: $420,000. Four Hundred Twenty Thousand and 00/100. Signed: Future Granger Graduate."

I also had a PowerPoint presentation like the one shown in figure 7.1, which was broken down into a number of slides so we could deal with each bubble one at a time. In this way, students would not be overwhelmed by the big picture until after they had seen each piece.

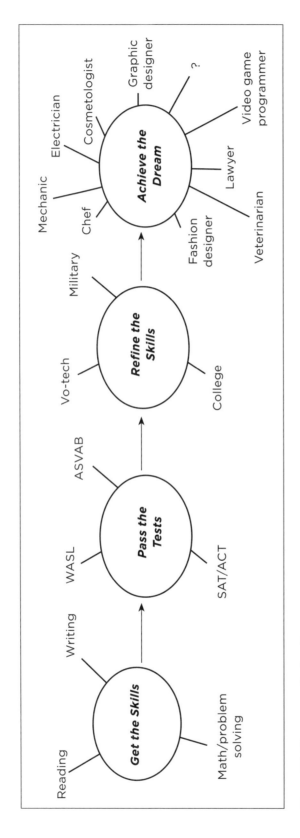

Figure 7.1: The power of education.

Once the students were seated in the gym, I addressed them: "A lot of people talk about the power of education. But what does that really mean? Today, I'm going to show you." I laid out my case that any dream was possible, but the key to any of those dreams lies in students taking their education seriously and developing their skills. We talked about how students needed to build up their basic skills not just to pass the WASL, but also so they could pass the tests that would allow them to get further training. Even students who weren't college bound still needed the skills to do well on the Armed Services Vocational Aptitude Battery (ASVAB) test if they wanted to take advantage of the military's training or on entrance exams into technical colleges. If students could not pass the tests, they could not develop the more specialized skills they needed to have the kind of job they wanted in the future. Education, particularly education that developed high-level skills in reading, writing, and math, had the power to make or break their future dreams. "That is the power of education, and it is available to every single one of you," I said. "There's no mystery about how you can get to your dreams. It all starts with getting the job done right here, right now, today and tomorrow, and one day at a time."

I then brought out the giant check and told the students the facts about the average income differential between high school graduates and nongraduates. That check was the equivalent of the traffic-safety certificates that I let my students hold in their hands before they had earned them. It was a physical symbol of a reality, a future reality that connected to their present reality. Just as I had told the students in my traffic-safety class, we were telling our kids that we were not going to send them out to take the tests of life unprepared. We knew how to prepare them; they just had to work with us. In time, the check, like the driver's license, would be theirs. It was a guarantee, a certain reward for their efforts.

The check was not the only visual I brought out at the assembly. On a table next to my podium sat a pile of something covered by a cloth. "Do you know how much money four hundred twenty thousand dollars is?" I asked the students. "What does it look like? How much would it weigh in your hands?" I lifted the cloth. Beneath it, stacked up like a ransom being paid to a kidnapper, was $420,000 in twenty-dollar bills. Well, sort of. Because there had not been a $420,000 line item for motivating students in my budget, I had my office staff copy the front side of a real $20 bill, substituting the words *Play Money* for the words *Twenty Dollars* that ran along the bottom edge. (Note: Do not try this at home! The Secret Service contacted me after word of my fake twenties was published in a newspaper. I did not know that the Secret Service was in charge of investigating counterfeiting. I know now! And I also now know that they are quite serious about doing their job. Be sure to read the rules the government requires you to follow if you are going to copy money.)

I invited students to come down after the assembly and look at the stacks of twenties, hold a stack in their hands, and feel the weight of it. I had also instructed our office staff to make extra copies of the fake twenties so the students could pick up one for themselves. I showed them that the back contained the phrase "Honor yourself and your family by valuing your education" and encouraged them to keep the fake money as a reminder. Judging by the run on the fake bills, the message got through.

Advertising

So I had delivered my message, but I didn't want it to be a one-time occurrence. I thought about how advertisers constantly try to keep their product on your mind through commercials, newspaper and magazine ads, and billboards. Look at the power of TV commercials, for example. Shortly after I arrived at Granger in 1999, a new TV commercial debuted. If you watched TV even a tiny bit from 2000 to the present, tell me what comes to mind when I say these two words: Jared and Subway. If it had not been for those TV ads showing pictures of an obese man and then a live shot of a trim man holding up comically large pants against his now-slender frame, we would have never heard of Jared Fogle from Indiana. But not only do we remember his name, we know his story. Who would have thought anyone could lose 240 pounds by eating at Subway? If our brains told us that eating fast food could not possibly help us successfully lose weight, the images in that advertisement told another part of us otherwise. Subway sales exploded, doubling in just a few years (York, 2008).

The $420,000 check, the stacks of money, and the value-your-education twenties were all advertisements, and advertising needs repetition to be effective. We had a laminated poster maker at the school, and I decided that we would wear out that machine by making our own billboards. I printed eleven-by-seventeen-inch versions of the check, and we hung them in the halls and in classrooms. Our little $420,000 check billboards reminded our students about the power of education and gave them a reason to do what we were asking them to do. There were certainly pressures from some of the students with their accusations of "schoolboy!" hurled at their former mates who were now trying to better themselves. But it is hard to argue with money, and we were building a pretty compelling and logical case, first with the assembly and then with our visuals, that education was the way for students to get what was theirs.

Struggles

Sometime after we posted our billboards, I noticed that someone had written on one of the large checks, "Time to GET HIGH!" I was unhappy that someone would take a positive message and trash it like that, but I knew we were in a fight.

We were not in a fight with students; we were in a fight with negative beliefs. Our students had developed negative beliefs about school, themselves as learners, and their futures. It took years of negative experiences and social conditioning for these beliefs to develop. Psychologists tell us that once a belief is established, to try to change it creates internal conflict, an internal fight. The old beliefs are not going to go quietly.

I knew many of our students were experiencing internal conflicts about what to believe. In a way, when the graffiti artist defaced our billboards, he had done a good thing. He brought the fight that was raging inside him and so many of our other students into the open. He brought it from the neighborhood of his heart and soul, and came and tagged our territory in retaliation for invading his turf. Once he declared war, he gave me the signal that it was time to push farther into enemy territory and confront negative beliefs that were hiding in the trenches of our students' psyches.

What I didn't understand was why the tagger had chosen to write, "Time to GET HIGH!" on the check, so I asked my advisory. What followed was very educational; my students explained all the reasons that 420 was a code word for "time to get high." I couldn't believe it! Out of all the numbers that some marijuana users could have picked, it just had to be the same as the number on our checks. Now what? Were we supposed to pull down all the checks and try something else because popular culture had already claimed our number for its own?

This was not the only struggle we faced in getting out our message about the power of education. A debate began when a staff member challenged me about some new information I had recently presented about the connection between a person's reading level and his or her average income. The data I presented showed both the average incomes of people of different reading skill levels and the average reading levels of people in different professions. As you would expect, the higher-income professionals, such as scientists, nurses, and executives, had higher reading levels than lower-income professionals like service workers, laborers, and construction workers. I was trying to encourage students by telling them that the more they improved their reading level, the more money they could make.

A well-respected paraeducator challenged me right after that assembly. "Mr. Esparza, what you said is not true. I have a very high reading level, but I don't make a lot of money."

"You're really good at your job with kids. Do you like what you do?" I asked. She told me that she loved it. "So even though a paraeducator doesn't make as much money as a scientist or a nurse or even a teacher, that's a pretty big benefit, to love what you do. Being a great reader has certainly helped you to do this job, right?" She agreed.

"As far as pay, don't you get benefits in addition to your salary?" I asked. "Don't you have a pretty good medical plan and paid sick days and even a retirement account?" Again, she agreed. "Well, in my book, that's a pretty good standard of living. For some people, money is the most important indicator of success. But I think a lot of people would say that being happy with your work and having benefits that take care of you when you're sick and money to live on when you retire, that's success to them. I'd say your reading skills have given you the power to choose a career that makes you happy and brings security, and those advantages are the most important things to you. If you didn't have great skills, you wouldn't be able to have this job. If you decided to do another job that paid more money and you thought it would make you happy, I bet you could go do it. Your reading skills certainly wouldn't hold you back."

Like her, students also challenged me that education did not always produce high income for people who were more educated. In response, I could have told them that these were just averages, that clearly there were exceptions to every rule, but by telling them that, I was giving them a loophole, and they could tell themselves they were the exception to the rule. I didn't want them to have a built-in justification when they did not feel like putting in the effort to improve their skills.

So I used the same line of reasoning I used with the paraeducator when students and staff challenged me about being too focused on money, and my argument seemed to make sense to all of them. The higher your skills, the more options you had to find the perfect mix of a salary you wanted, benefits that protected you, and deep satisfaction that you were doing something you loved.

I write about our struggles in changing the belief systems of our school community to help prepare you for two things. First, if people are opposing your message, you need to look deeply to find the real reason for the opposition. I believe the negative reactions to our positive messages were not just intellectual objections; they were actually emotional and psychological reactions. Our information was challenging people to push themselves into doing new things: to study harder, to teach more passionately, and to reach for their dreams. We were saying all of this was possible, but beliefs tied to people's past experiences and the unambitious side of themselves—something we all have inside us in one form or another—were rebelling against the idea. Their reactions were a defense mechanism to allow them to maintain the status quo. So it's important to have ready answers that address the actual issues behind their real objections, not just their intellectual objections.

The second reason for telling you about these struggles is to underscore, again, that this turnaround was a process. Change did not happen all at once, and it will not happen all at once in your school. The key for us was to keep struggling toward the goal and have faith that we would figure out what we needed to know as we went along. We hope your process will be faster by following our map, but do not be fooled into thinking that problems won't surface along the way. Rather, have faith that you will encounter no problems that you cannot eventually solve.

The Three Roads of Life

After I spent a long time processing our struggles, I planned another assembly to address the problems head-on. I had recently seen a movie titled *Domino* (Scott, 2005). In one scene, a wealthy family member explains to another character that there are three kinds of people in life, and that scene stuck with me and made me think. So when I stepped up in front of the student body packed into our gymnasium, I told them about my disappointment that someone would deface our fake checks because to me they weren't fake, they were real. There really was an earnings gap of $420,000 between graduates and nongraduates. I related how I had thought about changing the amount on the checks or simply getting rid of them altogether, but I just couldn't do it. Paraphrasing a line from the movie, I told them, "You know, there really are three types of people in the world: there's rich people, poor people, and people in the middle. That's reality. Can anyone prove me wrong?"

Not a single voice spoke up to challenge my statement.

"But how do people end up getting sorted out like that?" I continued. "Are they just born that way? Are some people just lucky and others aren't? No, people don't just wake up and find themselves somewhere in life. Life is a journey. Let me show you what leads to people ending up either rich, poor, or in the middle."

At this point, I unveiled the poster shown in figure 7.2.

Whatever my poster lacked in quality of design was more than made up for by its direct truthfulness. I asked students to consider which road their parents were on, giving examples of different jobs and income levels. At the time, I defined low income as making $15,000 or less per year, average income as $20,000 to $35,000, and good to great income as $40,000 and above. If students did not know how much money their parents made, I told them a secret that they weren't aware of: jobs don't just pay employees with a salary; they can also pay with benefits. You can pretty accurately tell which road someone is on by the benefits that come with his or her job.

"Do you know how much more of your income has to go to paying for medical costs when you don't have health insurance?" I asked. "People without medical insurance or dental insurance or vision insurance pay more when they have health issues than people who have insurance benefits. It might seem unfair, but you know what? That's the way the world works."

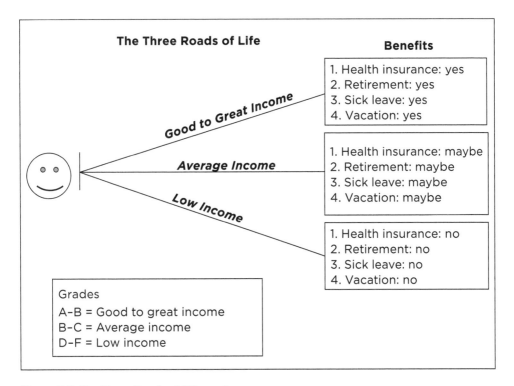

Figure 7.2: The Three Roads of Life poster.

I talked about my grandparents and how they lived after they retired. They did not have money to do anything because their only income was their Social Security checks, and it really bothered me to see them barely able to survive. I asked my students to think about their grandparents. Were they able to take trips, buy things for the grandkids, and help pay for their grandkids' college education? We talked about whether their parents lost their pay when they were sick and could not work. I asked the students if they ever got to go on vacations. Most had never thought about the fact that their family never went on vacations because doing so meant the parents would lose income while they weren't working.

By the time we finished this discussion, it was pretty easy for students to see which road their parents were on. For the majority of my students, it was the low road.

With this introduction, now it was easy to explain the power of education: "Each of you has the ability to choose where you end up, whether it is a high, average, or low income. You also have the ability to choose a job that makes you happy, which the smiling face on the poster represents. But you don't just end up with the income you want and the job you love by magic. You have to follow a road, and the road you take is directly tied to the grades you earn in school. Your grades are a direct reflection of how hard you are working to build your knowledge and skills. So if you want to earn a good to great income, you prepare yourself by getting all As and Bs. The road to getting a job with an average income and benefits is to get Bs and Cs in school. Although it may not seem like a choice, those of you who get Ds and Fs are actually choosing not to do the work, and the result is going to be that you will only have the skills to get the low-income jobs with no benefits. Show me your grades, and I will show you which road you are on.

"Here's the sad thing," I told them. "My grandparents were some of the most wonderful, most hardworking people I've ever known, but they were poor. They didn't even have the opportunity to go to school because their family pulled them out of school to work in the fields so the family would have enough money to survive. Every one of you listening to me right now is lucky that your parents have chosen to keep you in school, because once you leave school, your path is pretty much decided. My grandparents never had a chance to go back and build up their skills to get on a different road. They were stuck on the low road. The same is true for you. If you don't get the skills now, you'll probably be stuck on a path for the rest of your life. Which road are you on? Do you see where it ends up? Is that where you want to end up? If not, you need to change it while you still have time. Take advantage of all the help we're offering you to start moving toward where you want to go."

I also prepared for all the advisors a lesson plan that we went over in a faculty meeting/staff-development session so they would be ready to engage the students in a discussion. After a while, we added to the Three Roads of Life poster by placing tiny cutouts from an article titled "What People Earn," which *Parade* magazine prints every year. Each cutout showed a picture of a real person and his or her name and age, city, job title, and annual salary. I kept this copy in my office.

The power of that poster continued to serve me well for years. When struggling students were sent to my office, I asked, "Which road are you on?" I had the poster right there in my office to help our discussion. As we talked, I asked the student, "Where do you want to be?" I did not have to ask him or her, "Why are you doing this? Why are you acting this way?" and feel the defensiveness rise. I asked instead, "Why are you doing this to your future?" which was received more openly because it put me on the student's side. Together, we could look at the problem from the same side, shoulder-to-shoulder; we both wanted a bright future for the student; we both wanted the student to take the high road.

From there, we could deal with the root issues: "Do you know what you want to do for a career? What's getting in the way?" I also made full use of the other symbols we had created: the oversized checks and the value-your-education twenty-dollar bills. By this time, I had moved the stacks of $420,000 into a briefcase, which always sat right there next to my desk, and I opened it frequently, giving a tangible reminder to students who most needed it in those moments of turmoil or doubt.

I knew we were really changing belief systems when I heard fewer taunts of "schoolboy!" directed at students who were trying hard to improve their skills and more students saying, "I'm not going to be a loser." It was becoming less cool to adopt a slacker attitude, which our students now associated with being on the low road—and being on the low road meant you were a loser (not words I ever used with them, but their translation nonetheless). I think part of the reason for the old "schoolboy" taunt was that kids who were stuck in failure felt bad. By demeaning those students who were doing better than they were, these struggling students were really saying, "You're no better than me, Schoolboy." The combination of our whole system of motivational messages to work hard, interventions to give the support they needed to improve their academic skills, and the supportive three-way communication between school, home, and students was giving everyone success. When you feel successful, it is pretty hard to feel bad or to get tangled up in feelings of inferiority.

Sugarcoated or the Truth?

"I've got some new results about how well you're doing. Do you want me to sugarcoat it for you, or do you want me to tell you the truth?" This was a phrase that I found myself using a lot, from one-on-one conversations with students in my office to assemblies with the whole school. Invariably, I found that kids wanted me to give it to them straight. This preference gave me permission to share with students the data that we were using for decision making. I strongly believe that we need to share data about student performance not only with our teachers, but also with our students. After all, we were not performing some grand science experiment where we were using data to do work on students. We needed to work *with* students, not *on* them. How could our students be maximally effective as our partners if we did not share the data? I found this dose-of-truth data sharing to be particularly helpful, and motivational, when reviewing our state test scores with students.

One constant challenge we put before the kids was for them to examine how they were doing compared to their rivals, the Zillah Leopards from Zillah High School in Zillah, Washington. Zillah was only six miles from Granger, but it was a very different town from ours. Zillah High School had a much higher population of middle-class students and a much lower minority enrollment, and the school always seemed to kick our posterior whether it was in graduation rates, test scores, or on the scoreboards at sporting events. All the students and adults of both communities knew the score when it came to who was the top dog, and it had been a long time since Granger had come out favorably in its competition with Zillah.

This inferiority affected our kids deeply. The first time I told some students that one day they were going to get higher scores on the WASL test than Zillah, one of them looked at me and said point-blank, "Mr. Esparza, we're not as smart as they are." This negative outlook was the belief that our students had, and even though it wasn't true, it was based on years of experience and was deeply ingrained in them. In my first few years at Granger, I didn't dare to compare our test scores to Zillah's. It would have been too discouraging for our kids. Instead, I chose other communities whose scores were closer to ours to show them how they were doing.

The first time we did use the Zillah challenge in a class meeting with our sophomores, we had to get creative. Take a look at the data shown in table 7.1 to see the truth that we wanted to share with them in the fall of 2003.

Table 7.1: Granger-Zillah WASL Raw Score Comparison

School Year	Zillah Tenth-Grade Reading Scores	Granger Tenth-Grade Reading Scores
2000–01	68.2%	20.0%
2001–02	52.0%	34.2%
2002–03	71.0%	38.0%

If we had presented the data to our students like this, the first thing that would have hit them was the overall score differentials, which looked a lot like our basketball scores in the middle of the third quarter. Our kids would have been excited that Zillah went down in the 2001–02 school year while we went up, but then when they looked at 2002–03, they would have seen how Zillah shot ahead. Although we had improved a little, our students were likely to focus only on how much better Zillah did, and from there, it would have been easy for our students to fall back on their old belief that Zillah kids were just smarter. It had always been that way; it looked like it always would be.

We decided we needed to dig deeper into the data and show our students what was really happening. Not only was the data the truth, but also it had the kind of spin that helped our kids to see the enormous payoff for all their efforts. How much had our rivals improved compared to us? We knew that our sophomores who took the WASL in 2001 had scored 20 percent, but when they were seventh graders, they had scored only 2 percent. How much had their Zillah counterparts improved? (See table 7.2.)

Table 7.2: Granger-Zillah Seventh- to Tenth-Grade Improvement Scores

School Year	Zillah Seventh-Grade Reading Scores	Zillah Tenth-Grade Reading Scores	Zillah Percentage of Improvement	Granger Seventh-Grade Reading Scores	Granger Tenth-Grade Reading Scores	Granger Percentage of Improvement
2000–01	43.3%	68.2%	58%	2.2%	20.0%	809%
2001–02	35.8%	52.0%	45%	10.0%	34.2%	242%
2002–03	48.0%	71.0%	48%	10.8%	38.0%	252%

When we presented the data as shown in table 7.2, the results did not look (or feel) as bad. Yes, in the spring of 2001, Zillah beat our tenth graders 68 to 20, but we had improved 809 percent compared to their 58 percent improvement. That is the number I wanted our students to focus on. If we could continue to improve faster than the other guy, we would eventually pass him.

I wanted the students to really soak in this information, and that was not going to happen by talking at them with a humongous chart projected on the wall. I decided to break up the data and help students apply real-world reading and math skills while examining the scores. So when I presented the chart to the students—asking first if they wanted me to sugarcoat it or give them the truth—the first PowerPoint slide was only partially filled in, as shown in figure 7.3.

School Year	Zillah Tenth-Grade Reading Scores	Granger Tenth-Grade Reading Scores
2000–01	?	?

Figure 7.3: Slide 1: "Sugarcoated or the Truth?" presentation.

As I announced how Zillah had performed in 2001, I went to the next slide, which had the 68.2 percent filled in. Slide 3 showed the 20 percent that our sophomores had scored. I wistfully sighed and pointed out that it looked like Zillah had "wiped the floor with us" that year. I let the students feel a little uncomfortable, boo a little, and make comments such as "Thanks for the good news, Mr. Esparza" and "Don't be a hater." But then I continued by telling students that those two numbers were not representative of the full story. It was important for the students to understand where they started from if they wanted to know how far they had gone. Finally, I went to the fourth slide (see fig. 7.4 on page 156) that showed the expanded table with the 43.3 percent that our rivals scored in seventh grade filled in.

School Year	Zillah Seventh-Grade Reading Scores	Zillah Tenth-Grade Reading Scores	Zillah Percentage of Improvement	Granger Seventh-Grade Reading Scores	Granger Tenth-Grade Reading Scores	Granger Percentage of Improvement
2000–01	43.3%	68.2%			20.0%	

Figure 7.4: Slide 4: "Sugarcoated or the Truth?" presentation.

While students were viewing slide 4, I asked them how much Zillah's score had improved. Someone gave the answer as 24.9 points. I then pointed out how percentage of improvement yields a better comparison and asked for the formula for figuring the percentage of improvement. A student who thought he knew it came up to the board and wrote the formula. This exercise produced some disagreement, which I did not worry about. It was great to see students trying to work out how to do this real-world math.

When we finally got the formula (which, by the way, is tenth-grade score minus seventh-grade score divided by seventh-grade score multiplied by one hundred), I passed out calculators and let students try to figure out the percentage of improvement. After the invariable disagreements, I revealed the fifth slide, which showed the correct answer. The next slide showed the Granger seventh-grade score, and I had students calculate the percentage of improvement. Most students were unable to believe that the improvement was actually 809 percent. They had improved much more than Zillah had.

I followed this suspense-building process with each slide, letting the students work out the percentage of improvement each year, first for Zillah and then for Granger, before revealing the correct answer. This tactic kept their interest high and focused their attention on how much we were whomping Zillah with our percentage of improvement. This progress was something the students could control, and they knew it.

So our students got a good math and table-reading workout, while at the same time recognizing that their efforts were paying off. "Who do you think is working harder: the Zillah Leopards or the Granger Spartans?" I asked.

"The Spartans!" they yelled.

"Well, keep working," I told them. "If you keep going like this, you're going to pass Zillah soon." Then I reminded them of all the extra help we had available for them with our before- and after-school programs. If they wanted to put in the work, we would help them, and they would do amazing things.

If I had just shown the students only the raw number scores, they probably would never have believed that they could beat Zillah. But showing them how much they were really improving gave them faith. Their faith was well founded. Look at the scores over the next several years, as shown in table 7.3.

In 2006–07, we finally beat our rivals outright. I think there was as much excitement and pride as there would have been if we had beaten Zillah in football, maybe more, because *everyone* had participated in this victory, not just the boys on the team. We were all on the team.

Table 7.3: Granger's Improvement Trend Compared to Zillah's

School Year	Zillah Seventh-Grade Reading Scores	Zillah Tenth-Grade Reading Scores	Zillah Percentage of Improvement	Granger Seventh-Grade Reading Scores	Granger Tenth-Grade Reading Scores	Granger Percentage of Improvement
2003–04	27.4%	55.4%	102%	15.6	46.8	200%
2004–05	50.5%	72.5%	44%	8.1	61.3	657%
2005–06	39.1%	76.8%	96%	21.4	68.9	222%
2006–07	47.9%	70.5%	47%	21.2	76.5	261%
2007–08	60.4%	75.8%	25%	37.8	76.5	102%

Incidentally, by this time in my tenure at Granger High School, we were competing on a pretty equal par with our Zillah rivals on the athletic field, too. We actually beat them sometimes in arenas where we had seldom challenged them previously. Was it just a coincidence that this athletic success occurred at the same time we were showing our students what hard work could do? I will leave that one for you to decide.

We used this same strategy at the beginning of each year in a whole-school assembly when we announced how the various classes had performed on the WASL. We tried to make the results dramatic and competitive, like a pep assembly.

"Where are the seniors?" I asked. (Cheers rained down from the class of 2004.)

"When you seniors first began here as freshmen, you started preparing for the WASL. When you took the test as seventh graders, you scored . . ." I paused dramatically while I reached over to reveal the PowerPoint slide, "ten percent in reading." (Laughter and boos roared from the crowd as they saw the stubby little 10 percent bar on the bar graph.)

"Now, hold on!" I said. "Wait 'til you see where you went from there. The class that came right before you, the class of 2003, scored 20 percent in reading on the sophomore WASL." (Boos now from the class of 2004 as the PowerPoint slide showed the bar on the graph for the previous year dwarfing their class's seventh-grade score.)

"But you just had to show them up, didn't you? You worked hard; you did your job; and when you took the WASL reading test in your sophomore year, you got . . ." (I ever-so-slowly reached to change the PowerPoint slide.)

"Thirty-four point two percent!" (Wild cheering, not only from the class of 2004, but also from the other classes and even from the teachers.)

I continued with the juniors, showing their improvement from seventh grade (10.8 percent) to tenth grade (38 percent). The juniors had topped the senior class's WASL score in reading by 4 percent. We celebrated the four-point improvement and the fact that we as teachers and students had gotten smarter about how we prepared and had built on the success of the seniors and everything we had learned together. In this way, improvement was not only about competition, but also about collaboration. We made clear the legacy that each class left for the next one, lessons learned that paved the way for each succeeding class to take the baton and run faster and farther. We were all Granger Spartans, and we were all on the same team.

I continued the presentation, showing the sophomores and freshmen their scores as seventh graders (15.6 percent and 8.1 percent, respectively), revealing one bar at a time until the slide looked like the one shown in figure 7.5.

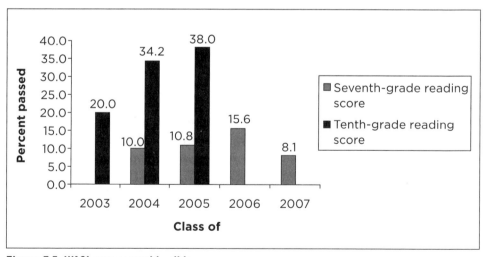

Figure 7.5: WASL pep assembly slide.

We talked about students' responsibilities to themselves, to their futures, to their families, and to their classes to beat the scores of the previous class. We talked about how we, as teachers, were getting smarter in helping them achieve their goals, because we had been working hard at it. We told students about the Rewire and Read-a-Lot programs, and how we would be talking a lot about reading. I warned them that they had better know what their reading level was when I came around and asked them about it in the cafeteria at lunch, and I told them they had better be able to tell me what they were doing to improve it.

This dialogue was the kind of tell-it-like-it-is, reality-based conversation that we engaged in with our students. When we gave students the choice to hear the sugarcoated version or the truth, they chose the truth. It was not shameful to talk about low reading levels; it was empowering, because we were basically saying, "Here you are now. Here's where you want to be. Now, how are we going to get there?" Truth was not a weapon that we used to bash egos. Truth was a map that, when we linked it to the hard work done collaboratively with people who cared about their success, would produce positive results and would get students to where they wanted to go. Indeed, the classes of 2006 and 2007 each beat the preceding classes, scoring 46.8 percent and 61.3 percent, respectively, on their tenth-grade tests.

If we want to start a revolution of learning in our schools, we cannot afford to withhold data from our students.

Calling in the National Guard

In addition to the efforts we were making to connect to students' realities about what they wanted in life and how they were going to get there, we tried to involve as many outside organizations as possible. If an organization had a hand out to us and if they were about helping students envision and prepare for the future, then we gladly joined hands and partnered with them.

For example, the Army National Guard sponsored a fitness competition that the physical education teacher brought to my attention. Obviously, that organization wanted to promote physical fitness and at the same time meet students who were physically fit and motivated by physical challenges to talk to them about a possible future in the military. Some educators might have personal objections to military recruiting at schools or even the military in general. I strongly believe that it is not our job to limit options for our students' futures, but rather to open all the options. By opening up all the options, students will have a much better chance of finding a career that excites them, a career that gives them direction and motivates them to work hard to prepare for it. So I told the recruiters to make sure to emphasize how the students needed to work hard in school to develop the skills they would need to be successful for different jobs in the military, and our students joined the fitness competition. Not only did some of the students end up being interested in the military as a potential career, but also our school got so motivated by the challenge of competing against other schools (thanks mainly to our tough-as-nails physical education teacher) that they won the competition against all the other schools in our valley for three straight years! Don't tell me that success didn't help many of our students' beliefs in themselves.

Our school continued to work with the army, the marines, and the other branches of the military. We partnered on both formal activities that the military representatives set up and the informal opportunities we created for them at our school, such as working alongside our students to paint our school or providing the grills and the meat for a Senior Appreciation Day barbeque.

Calling in the Colleges

Because we were a school with high poverty and a high enrollment of students of color, we were a natural target for colleges that wanted to develop greater diversity on their campuses. Our students had no concept of what it was like to go to college. We determined at one point that 70 percent of their parents had not even graduated from high school. College to these students was as disconnected from their reality as it had been from mine, where not a single person who showed up at our family barbeques had ever attended college.

As part of changing our students' internal beliefs, we didn't just hold college-recruitment days at the high school, during which college recruiters came and did presentations about their schools. We actually took our students to the colleges for field trips and spent hours walking around the campuses, attending special presentations, which the minority recruitment offices usually set up, and talking to real college students. We wanted to motivate our students to work hard in order to get to college and to begin to visualize themselves as college students. Only when they were able to clearly imagine themselves attending college would they begin to believe that postsecondary education was really possible. An important side effect of our trips was that our students found out by talking to college students that college was fun. This positive social interaction convinced our students even more that college was somewhere they wanted to be and that all the hard work to get there would be worth it.

We also partnered with organizations such as GEAR UP, a collaborative effort of our state's Higher Education Coordinating Board and the governor's office, the College Success Foundation, and others, to prepare low-income kids for college. Although we already had after-school tutoring programs in place, we were not about to turn down the offer from GEAR UP to run its program alongside ours. The staff GEAR UP provided and the activities the organization had designed didn't cost us any more time or money, and they made a huge difference in motivating and preparing our kids.

You Gotta Be Committed!

What does it mean to be committed? Try buying a car. You promise to make all of your monthly payments when you sign your name on the dotted line. If you do not honor your commitment, a visit from the repo man will not be far behind. Contracts are not new in education. For years, behavior contracts have been in use with students who need help controlling their impulses. We simply tried to extend this idea of contracts and commitments into the larger arena of student achievement. We wanted to provide a structure to help students be more self-disciplined and create a culture that supported hard work and achievement.

We implemented this structure as described in chapter 3. The personalized education *plan* wasn't just a personalized education *nice idea*. It was a contract. When students, teachers, and parents signed their names to the plan, they were committing to doing what the plan said. Each party witnessed the others sign. This witnessing of signatures was part of the social contract that helped ensure commitment from all parties. Like a lawyer in a courtroom, I was not averse to pulling out a contract in a moment of disagreement and asking, "Is that your signature on this contract? If you signed it, why aren't you following through with what you said you would do?"

The Pledge

We also tried to find other ways to build commitment into our programs and goals. In December 2003, *Parade* magazine published an article titled "Your Mind Can Map Your Destiny" (Carson, 2003). I was fascinated by the story of Ben Carson, the director of the Division of Pediatric Neurosurgery at Johns Hopkins University. He was raised in poverty by an African American single mother, first in Detroit and later in Boston. The article says he started out with "terrible grades, anger and low self-esteem," but he made a decision to change the direction of his life at the age of ten with the help of his mother's "firm hand." In a year and a half, Carson went from the bottom of his fifth-grade class to the top of his seventh-grade class by "devouring book after book." Looking back at this decision with the benefit of his current expertise in neuroscience, Carson proclaims that humans are unlike any other creature. Unlike animals, we humans do not have to be "victims of circumstance" because our brains' frontal lobes enable us to analyze problems, create solutions, and plan for the future.

Carson's message provided a new twist to the one we were trying to get across to our students, namely, that if they would become voracious readers, they could have anything they wanted in a career. He was proof of someone who had done just that, and he provided some of the newest science behind why it was possible for students to become the people they dreamed of becoming. I wanted our students to read this article and talk about it, but I wanted this idea to stick. I wanted there to be some sense of commitment for them, to make a decision like the one that Carson had made as a boy.

In searching for a way to create a symbol of commitment, I thought about the dollar bills that some businesses proudly display on their walls: the first dollar they ever made. What if at the time students made the decision to change their lives through reading, we gave them a special dollar to commemorate their decision? That dollar, the first of many they would earn through the power of their education, would serve as a reminder of their decision.

I decided the Sacagawea dollar coin would make a special keepsake; it had come out a few years earlier but was still relatively rare to see in circulation. Even the subtle message on the coin of a poor native girl who contributed to great explorations through her intelligence and commitment was a welcome message. So I went to the bank and purchased more than three hundred of the coins, along with special cases to protect them.

I told the students about Carson's amazing story and emphasized that the most amazing thing about it was that his story could be any of theirs. The same powers of a brilliant brain that he carried inside his poor boy's skull were locked away inside their brains. Reading was the key that would unlock it. If students chose to do what he did, they could have what he had and become what he became. Next, we talked about the concept of your first dollar, something you earned by the sweat of your brow and kept as a reminder of where you started from and where you were going. Then I challenged the students to make a commitment to be the captain of their own ship, the master of their own destiny, by using their minds to steer their course and by filling their minds with the great thoughts found in books. If they were willing to sign a pledge to create their destiny through the power of reading and self-education, then we would give them one of the Sacagawea dollars to commemorate their decision.

We made copies of Carson's article and had the students read the article and then fill out a questionnaire. Afterward, the advisors led discussions on the article and the students' answers to the questions. These discussions were a good way for the students to grapple with and personalize the ideas that Carson posed. Were they held back by their socioeconomic status or their race? What were the things that got in the way of their education?

Finally, we gave students the opportunity to sign the pledge of commitment to their education. This process took place in the social context of the advisories and only after the students had processed the messages of the article and personalized them. We made clear that signing the pledge was not mandatory. In fact, we didn't want students to sign the pledge if they were not willing to make an honest commitment. To those who did, the advisors handed out the special commemorative coins.

In or Out

A few years after our Sacagawea-dollar campaign, I stopped by the classroom of our health teacher and noticed something new. Right in the middle of the doorway of her classroom, she had a line taped on the floor. Borrowing an idea for commitment that she had heard from her coaching hero, Pat Summitt, she pasted a sign on her door that said, "By stepping over this line, you are making a commitment to learn." She talked to her students about the message and told them that they were either in or out. If they were in her room, they were going to work hard to learn. If they didn't want to learn, they couldn't come in the room.

I loved the idea and wanted to spread it to the whole school with just one change. I can still remember my college wrestling coach talking to me about keeping my head up. To him, body language could either help or hinder your achievement. He noticed that I would sometimes walk around with my eyes cast downward. "Are you looking for quarters on the ground?" he would ask me.

"No," I'd reply.

"Then look up," he'd tell me. "You're not going to find what you're looking for down on the ground. Lift your chin up and be proud of who you are and where you're going."

This little secret of body language, that your path tended to follow where you were looking, stuck with me. Our students came mostly from impoverished, minority backgrounds and felt they might not be able to compete in the majority culture. We couldn't have them looking down because they weren't going to find what they were looking for there.

So I announced to the staff at a faculty meeting what I wanted to do. Above every classroom door, I wanted to put a sign that read, "By passing through this door, you are making a commitment to learn." The staff liked this, so we discussed how to present the idea to the students in our advisories. We had mostly gotten past the days when taunts of "schoolboy!" were common, but this action was taking our idea of commitment to the next level. After planning as a staff, individual advisors talked with their classes.

Advisors discussed with students the things that would get in the way of their wanting to learn, such as an emotional upset or a vexing problem, and talked about ways to resolve such issues or put those problems aside while they learned. Students were free to go to the counselor instead of entering the classroom if they felt it was a good idea. They could take a few moments as a time-out in class and write down their thoughts and feelings about a problem if they needed to before continuing. And if problems were getting in the way too often, then the student would need to come in after school to make up the time or schedule time with his or her advisor, the counselor, or even a friend to talk about things and figure out a solution.

In essence, we were all agreeing that real life has a tendency to get in the way of our goals sometimes, but we have to rise above the obstacles. We especially have to honor ourselves and others inside the walls of the classrooms and make them sacred spaces where learning was the primary purpose. If we let too many of the obstacles into the room with us, we could lose that sacred space. A few people who were not focused on learning could drag everyone down. We all depended on each other to do our part and stay focused on learning so that everyone learned together.

Man Up!

I loved to play basketball with our students. In fact, when we remodeled our high school, I made sure that we poured money into constructing a central courtyard so the students could get outside of the cafeteria during good weather to eat lunch and play together. We had a couple of basketball hoops and a volleyball court, along with a number of benches and places for kids to hang out. While Will would play volleyball with students and other teachers, I would often play basketball. Playing with kids is a great way to build rapport and build a stronger connection.

A common phrase in basketball is to "man up," which means to play defense such that every person on your team chooses a player on the other team that he or she will guard. It is man-to-man defense, and you are responsible for keeping track of your man; otherwise, the team will suffer.

So far, our strategies for motivation have been about big messages and initiatives, and those larger strategies are certainly important. But there is an underlying approach that I think is equally as important, and it's captured in the phrase *man up*. No matter how many motivational assemblies we have or how many innovative strategies we apply to inspire students, it all comes down to caring for individuals—to keeping track of your man—so the team doesn't suffer.

I made a commitment to myself early on that I would try to touch one student's life every day. Although I had days when my other responsibilities got in the way and it didn't happen, I had other days when my responsibilities made sure that interaction happened, such as when a student landed in my office due to poor performance in the classroom. At those times, my philosophy to man up would help me focus on understanding the student's predicament and how he or she could make more positive choices instead.

But I didn't want to just be reactive, dealing with students only after they were in trouble. I put myself purposefully out there and kept my eyes open for ways to touch lives. Playing basketball opened up chances afterward to ask how classes were going. And supervising the cafeteria didn't have to be just policing the kids. I started to use the time to talk to students.

One of my commitments to man up was to know every student's name and his or her reading level. I studied photos and constantly tried to call students by their name when I saw them. The astonished reactions I sometimes got—How do you know my name?—were not only rewarding, but also told me that I was doing something important. I was also quick to ask students at lunch what their reading level was. If they didn't know, and if I couldn't remember, I had a notebook with me that listed the reading level of every student in the school. If they were not reading on grade level, I would ask them how Rewire, our reading intervention, was going or what book they were currently reading.

I was firmly convinced that reading held the key to unlock our students' future success, especially if they had to develop perseverance in the pursuit of improving weak reading skills. If they could overcome that handicap, they were building two strengths: reading skill and tenacity in reaching goals. So I was not shy in bringing up the conversation. If students had improved their reading score, I tried to let them know that I knew about it before they shared it with me, which demonstrated even more to them how much I cared about how well they could read. If one of them broke the news to me that he or she had improved, the conversation gave me the chance to publicly celebrate with them and their small circle of friends. There was never any lack of certainty that their principal thought their reading skills were important.

Other social ties became a force for change by using the man-up philosophy. I remember talking to a student and her boyfriend about how their reading was going. Both of them were in English 2, meaning that they were reading somewhere between a fifth-grade and an eighth-grade level. The girl told me that she was doing really well, that her reading had really been improving. In fact, she was doing so well that she thought she was going to test out of the class and be moved to our on-level English 3 class, with the rest of the sophomores. But—and here she started to tease a little—she didn't think her boyfriend was going to make it. His reading had not improved as much as hers, so he was going to be kept behind in English 2. Well, her boyfriend was going to have none of that! When he heard her saying that, he basically told her, "No way! I'm going to work hard, and I'm going to make it." He did start working hard, and although he couldn't catch up to her by semester time, he did improve enough by the end of the year to move out of English 2. Would he have made it without the gentle social pressure of a goading girlfriend? That I do not know, but I do know that my decision to man up and to ask kids about the really important parts of their lives played a part. If I had not brought up the subject with the two of them, it may never have come up. Somehow, I don't think reading skill was the most important thing on the minds of two sixteen-year-old lovebirds!

Replacing Negative Traditions

You have probably heard that if you place a frog in a shallow pan of water that is boiling, the frog will instinctively react and jump out of the pan. But if you put the frog into a pan of soothingly warm water and ever so gradually heat it up, the frog will be unaware of the danger of the increasingly hot water until it is too late. By the time it realizes something is amiss, its physical systems are too compromised to be able to jump, and it ends up as frog soup. I have never tested this idea with an actual frog, and I do not know anyone who actually has, but I believe it. It is what I encountered when I came to Granger. Some of the pans of water I stepped into made me instantly recoil because I saw the danger, yet I was amazed to find our community, both students and full-grown adults, happily stewing in their own soup.

No More Skip Days

One negative tradition I had to address surfaced near graduation time during my first year as principal at Granger. Our Associated Student Body vice president was in our in-house suspension room because of a disciplinary infraction. He was not what most people think of as a typical student body leader. At the time, he was already a father. The mother of his child was our ASB president. This situation was common knowledge throughout the school, and there was no sense of shame or embarrassment about this. I considered this young man to be a leader of a negative gang of students. They didn't have a color or a gang sign, but they definitely had a shared belief system. To them, to live was to party. School was not important to their lives. It was nothing to cheat on their homework or to do whatever they needed to do to just get the grade and pass the class so they could graduate. School was a game, something they endured in order to get to the parties.

Our seniors had a tradition of Senior Skip Day. Apparently, this custom was one area in which the negative gang had aspirations of excellence. Two weeks earlier, they had held their *second* skip day because one day was not enough for this party-hardy crew. Unfortunately for them, secrecy was not a shared gang value, and adults in the community soon got word of what these students had done. The kids had skipped school and gone to the mountains to a cabin that one of our school board members owned. When he found out about it, he drove up to the cabin and found a large number of drunken students. At that point, he called the superintendent, and they decided they had better get a school bus to bring all these kids home, because they didn't want anyone killing themselves trying to drive home.

The two weeks following were a circus—complete chaos. We had to figure out which students had been drinking and which had not. Various angry parents were either in states of denial or actively protecting their kids. Many of the students were athletes, and their drinking made them ineligible to compete in sports. By the time we completed our inquiry, our track team was decimated, and our baseball team no longer had enough athletes left to continue their season, so the remaining games were simply forfeited.

So as I walked past this young man sitting in his isolated cubicle in our suspension room, I asked him his thoughts about what had happened. What did he think about all the people who got hurt? About the sports seasons that were ruined? About all the angry parents? I was completely taken aback when he showed no remorse. There was no acceptance whatsoever of the suffering that was his legacy. His response told of a different legacy.

"You know, there has never been a senior class that has had three skip days. We're going to be the first class ever to do three," he said.

As sad as his response was, it was not so different from that of some of the parents in the community. "It's just the way things have always been," some muttered. "You've got to let kids be kids," they protested when the suspensions came down. And worst of all: "Things were just fine until you had to come here and go sticking your nose into things."

I had a newsflash for these parents: things were not just fine. It was not fine to have the role models of your school cheating on tests or skipping school and defying authority just to party. None of that was going to lead to productive lives. And had anybody looked at our test scores?

You can only change the world one person at a time, so I dealt with the person in front of me in that moment. "Doesn't it ever get old, all the partying?" I asked. "How many times have you gotten drunk and partied 'til you puked? Isn't it pretty much the same old thing after awhile? Don't you ever wish for something new, something that was fun and exciting and not the same old, same old?"

"I don't know," he replied.

"Well, have you ever been on a boat?" I asked. He never had. He had never gone inner tubing behind a boat or water-skiing. I had an idea.

"What if instead of the same old tired thing, we substitute your third skip day for something nobody at Granger has ever done? We'll go down to a park on the Columbia River. I'll bring my boat, and I'll take you and all the seniors out for rides, and you can go tubing and try to water-ski. We'll have a big barbeque and all kinds of food, and we'll play softball and basketball and volleyball and have fun all day. What would you think about that?'

"Hmm . . . I'd have to think about it," he replied.

"All right, you think about it and talk to some of your buddies. I'd be willing to do this if you promise to make it your third skip day. But because you've already skipped two days of school and I can't justify you missing any more, we'd have to do it on a Saturday."

"Saturday? I don't know," he said.

"Well, talk to everybody and see what they want. They might never get a chance to do something like this again. You'll have the rest of your life to party. Who wants to pass up the opportunity to do something that's never been done before?"

So this young man did talk to his friends. They were interested enough that we had a formal meeting with the senior class to talk about it. After discussion, they voted to forgo their third skip day and replace it with Senior Appreciation Day, a name that put a positive spin on the day. I worked hard to put the pieces in place because I needed to build trust with the students. I got some teachers to agree to chaperone and some AmeriCorps volunteers, too. I got the National Guard to supply an army-sized barbeque and the meat for hamburgers and hot dogs. The superintendent agreed to make the outing an official field trip, so the buses were paid for, and we were able to take our school's sports equipment.

The first Senior Appreciation Day was a rousing success. Word spread about what a great time they had on our trip. Our whole high school and our whole community were buzzing about it. By the next fall, all I had to do was mention to the senior class that they could have a Senior Appreciation Day if they would give up any skip days, and they immediately and wholeheartedly agreed.

A new, positive tradition was born. This progress may seem like a small thing, but I disagree. By the reactions of all the students and parents in the wake of skip day number two, I could see that, traditionally, some members of our community did not take school very seriously. We were going to change that mind-set.

I wanted our students to know that partying felt best when it was done as a celebration of achievement. If the world that our kids grew up in did not support this more positive belief about partying, then we would have an awfully hard time getting anyone to work hard for future dreams. "Laugh today, cry tomorrow," a popular motto of the Latino gangs in our area, could not be our motto. Our changing of the Senior Skip Day tradition represented an assault on all of that negativity. We were challenging beliefs face to face, forcing people to see things in a new way. For these reasons, I see changing negative traditions into positive ones as a necessary tool in changing the beliefs and behaviors of a school community.

A Band of Colors

We also changed traditions in ways that were not as immediately noticeable. When we strictly enforced the ban on gang clothing, we sent the message that gangs were not the road to a good future.

We fought the baggy pants, the oversized hoodies, the long belts, and, most importantly at that time in our school, the bandanas. These red or blue symbols of which gang you were with or wanted to be with were probably the most inflammatory pieces of clothing our kids could wear. And wear them they did—until we started to confiscate them.

At this point, we did something a little different from most other schools. Instead of throwing away the bandanas, I collected them. I tied each bandana to the end of a long chain of bandanas I had confiscated, alternating red and blue so that each color touched the other color. I hung the chain on one wall of my office. If the timing was right when I confiscated a bandana, I brought the student into my office and tied it to the chain right before his or her eyes; otherwise, I invited the student in later, when it didn't interrupt class time. The effect of seeing his or her bandana tied to another gang's bandana was powerful. "Why do you do that? Why do you disrespect us like that?"

"I'll tell you why I do that," I said. "I want to keep track of how many kids I'm losing. Every one of those bandanas represents one person I've lost to poverty or drugs or violence. I hate losing even one person, so when I look at that chain, it makes me want to fight all the harder so we don't lose any more. It makes me want to fight so I don't lose you."

"Do you know why you guys use colors?" I asked. The student never had much of an answer, so I provided some history. "Colors were used by armies so they could tell each other apart. Back in the old days, people fought with the people who lived near them because they didn't have fighter jets to go thousands of miles away to fight. So the people they ended up fighting looked a lot like them. It was hard to tell them apart. How could they keep from shooting their own guys? They used flags of a certain color so that when they looked across a field they would know whether the people they saw were on their side. Then they would wear clothing of a certain color so that when they got closer they could tell who their enemy was.

"Look at you guys today. You're so alike that you can't tell each other apart, so you use colors. But you've got the wrong enemy, and that's why I'm taking away your colors. Like this string of bandanas, you guys are all actually connected. Your common enemy is your lack of knowledge, the lack of skills that will keep you not only from making a good living for yourself, but also from making the world a better place. The gangs tell you that if you join together, you can make a good life for yourself, but gangs aren't out to make the world a better place. They say you have to hurt someone else in order to get what you want; it's us against those other guys. That's not the kind of world I want to live in. I don't want you taking something away from me or my kids or my neighbor's kids or anyone. There's too much hate and hurt in the world. The only way to beat it is to realize that we are all the same color underneath.

"So I'm glad you want to fight. I want you to look at this chain of bandanas and think about who your real enemy in this world is. Don't waste your time fighting the wrong enemy. Choose your enemy wisely and choose to fight it."

This is how we turned a tradition, the wearing of colors to separate and inflame, into a symbol that communicated the truth. We gave an old symbol an alternative meaning that our gang kids may not have found easy to accept, but the story was certainly hard for them to forget once they had heard it.

In addition to banning gang attire, our custodial crew painted over graffiti as soon as it appeared, and I spent time consistently chasing away out-of-school gang members from the front of our building when school was let out each day. All of these actions comprised the first half of our efforts to change the belief that gangs were just a normal part of life.

The second half of our efforts focused on our commitment to actually getting results with our students. As students began to experience success, they found it easier to believe our message about the power of education. Sharing the data with them, giving them support, predicting a positive future if they would work hard, and then showing them how they had improved—in doing this, we were promoting a positive way of life, not simply banning the negative influences of the gangster way of life. We wanted them to say yes to an educated life, not just say no to gangs. Without the positive action, we would not have had the alternative reality for our students to grab ahold of once we had asked them to let go of the gangs.

Changing the Reputation

I believe all of us are affected by what others think about us—some of us more than others, but all of us to some degree. For example, students are affected by what teachers think about them. The classic example of this comes from the experiment by Robert Rosenthal and Lenore Jacobson (1968) published in *Pygmalion in the Classroom*. In this study, teachers were told that 20 percent of their students were ready to make a growth spurt on their achievement that year, and that prediction was based on an intelligence test that all of the students had taken. Although the 20 percent of students were, in fact, randomly selected and no test indicated that they were expected to have a growth spurt, those students' performance at the end of the year outpaced that of students who had not been labeled as anything special. The conclusion, then, is to say that what teachers believe about their students is important, and that being the case, I wanted our teachers to think of our students as something special.

But what students think about their teachers has also been shown to affect student performance. One example from research is Robert Feldman and Thomas

Prohaska's study (1979) in which students were taught two minilessons and then questioned about what they had learned. Half of the students were told before the class that the teacher was very effective and likable. The other half was told that the teacher was boring and bumbling. After the minilessons, the students who were told the teacher was excellent scored 65.8 percent on a test of the subject. Students who expected the teacher to be an idiot scored 52.2 percent. In both cases, the same teacher taught the same lesson.

I wanted our teachers and our students to have high expectations of each other, but this was not some psychological experiment. This was the real world, where expectations had been built on past experiences. Where expectations were low, they were easily traced to a shared history of low performance. Our school had a bad reputation.

Reputations are built on actions. We were definitely taking steps to do things differently from in the past. Consequently, our reputation would change eventually. But the process of changing our reputation, like the process of rebuilding trust between two people once it's been broken, takes time, and we didn't have time to wait. We needed help to speed up the process of building a new reputation. That meant getting the good news about what we were doing out to the public. If people didn't know what we were doing, they couldn't care about it, and it would be as if what we did hadn't really happened. I wanted our students and teachers to start hearing from community members that they had heard good things about the school.

When we did the campaign to visit all five hundred homes in our district, I made sure to call the newspapers. The newspapers had printed a lot of negative content about our school and our community. They had reported the murder of one of our students in the parking lot, publicized day after day the brutal murder of another family, and published our brutally low test scores for everyone to see. So I told the editors we were doing something unique and that the community deserved to know about it. They were happy to come out, take photos, and run a huge story on our efforts. I was amazed at all the positive comments I heard about that article, and I remained determined to keep providing the good news.

I started calling the papers about every bit of good news I could find. I probably got turned down about 75–80 percent of the time, but I kept trying. When we started our new conference system, the newspaper ran a big article. That story led to a request from a TV station for an interview, so I started to forward news ideas to the TV and radio stations. I spent time getting to know reporters at these media outlets and building a rapport with them so they would become my willing co-conspirators in changing our reputation at Granger.

When we hosted a Make a Difference Day, during which our students volunteered to do something positive in the community, we got TV coverage and pictures in the paper of the marines working with our students to paint our school. When our students met a challenge to read fourteen thousand books, Will and I, along with another teacher, Lynn Woodyard, made good on our promise to climb a fourteen-thousand-foot mountain. And we made sure to invite all the media to publicize that our high school students had climbed a metaphoric mountain every bit as real as the physical one that the three of us climbed. They had each read an average of forty-five books in a little more than a year, something pretty phenomenal for high school students who previously hated to read. When we won our first National Model High School award and our state schools' superintendent came to our school to present our award at an assembly, reporters were present.

The community was definitely hearing about our success, and our students heard about it, too. It's one thing for teachers or a principal to say that a school and its students are doing well, but when you read that in the newspaper or see it on TV, well, that's even better. I made sure to announce to students when a news article or TV report would appear, especially when that news was republished in the *Seattle Times*. Our students began to develop a sense that what they were doing was special. After all, if the state's biggest newspaper published it, it must be true!

Besides our big achievements, I also pushed stories about individual students who had persisted and overcome obstacles by taking advantage of the supports we offered them. One such case resulted in a great story of two young men going to college because they refused to let their past mistakes hold them back, doing instead the hard work necessary to make another attempt at getting their diplomas.

We could have kept quiet and gone humbly about our business, never trumpeting our accomplishments or the good things we saw on a daily basis, but what good would that have done our students? We wanted to accelerate the process of change in our school. Formerly, our students and teachers heard the community around us express negative opinions about them. Those negative opinions had sabotaged their efforts to do better in years past. Now, as news about our results was reported, a snowballing effect of positive energy fueled our efforts to improve. I have heard it said that a secondhand compliment is the best kind to get—that's the kind of compliment where someone you know says he or she heard someone else saying something nice about you. The secondhand compliment feels especially good because you know the person relaying the compliment to you didn't have to tell you, and the person who said the nice thing about you originally didn't know you were going to hear about it; that individual just honestly thought something nice about you. In the same way, I think our students felt the compliment to be much truer and much better when they heard me say, "You know what the newspaper said about you?" than it felt when I told them what I said about them.

Celebrating Success

I believe that celebrating success is important. Turning around a school is hard work for teachers, students, and administrators. In some ways, a school turnaround can be a never-ending struggle. It is important to stop occasionally, to look back at how far you have come, and to celebrate the journey.

Numbers do not lie. Our school was achieving real results. So I shared that information frequently with students and staff at assemblies. Sometimes it was just the data. Sometimes it was stories of what individual students had accomplished. The year that we had a student go from a third-grade reading level to an eleventh-grade reading level in one year, you better believe we told his story in front of the whole school. We let them know that this student had decided to read hour after hour on his own, and look at what had happened as a result.

We also held assemblies during which we handed out Accelerated Reader awards for students who read the most books. To get more students on the honor roll, I created new honor rolls for students with a 2.0 grade point average and above and a 2.5 and above. We phased these awards out eventually, but we had so few students making the 3.0 and 3.5 honor rolls at the start that most of our students didn't know what it felt like to be on the honor roll. We wanted students to have that feeling and to like it so that success would breed success.

One of our students' favorite celebrations was when I asked them to come to the cafeteria during advisory so I could share some good news with them. After I delivered the news, our kitchen staff served up root beer floats for everyone.

Going to the movies was a special event for many of our students. So when a particularly inspirational movie was playing, I used it as a celebration for our students taking the WASL tests (or the Iowa Tests of Educational Development that our freshmen took). If students worked hard and didn't give up or quit early when they got frustrated on the tests, they would get tickets to see movies such as *Coach Carter* (Gale, Robbins, Tollin, & Carter, 2005) or *Akeelah and the Bee* (Fishburne, Ganis, Hult, Llewelyn, Romersa, & Atchison, 2006).

Each fall, our school hosted a dinner to celebrate the scores our students had received on the WASL. I invited all of the students who had taken the test and their parents to join us in our cafeteria. I hired our kitchen staff (through parental involvement funds), and the cheerleaders used the event as a fundraiser, selling hamburgers and french fries to the attendees. I gave our teachers the royal treatment, buying them steak and salmon as a way to thank them for all of their hard work.

All of these events were celebrations, not rewards. The rewards were what the kids had achieved. These celebrations gave us the opportunity to verbalize these rewards and to talk about how the students, teachers, and parents were proving a lot of people wrong. A lot of doubters remained nonetheless, but they would not be able to doubt much longer. It didn't matter where students came from or what color their skin was or how little money they had. The power of education could take them anywhere if only they committed to doing the work. We celebrated the very real results that everyone's commitment was bringing about. Our history was being rewritten from the inside out.

Chapter 8

WILL THE GRANGER MODEL WORK IN ANY SCHOOL?

That wouldn't work in my school because . . .

Your school might be too big. It might be too urban. Your teachers' union might be too powerful and your superintendent too weak. These are not my own words; people across the country have used these excuses to tell me they cannot do in their school what we did because their circumstances are just too different from ours.

Our system is not some ivory-tower scheme. Our system was proven under some of the toughest conditions, and now you have the road map. It did not cost us anything above ordinary operating costs, so money is not the problem in implementing the system. We used our existing hours of work, rearranged to offer a little more flexibility to put our system in place, so time is not the problem either. It is not a question of know-how. The real question is this: do you have the will to take simple actions that get right to the reason behind why so many students are failing?

If you are a superintendent, talk to your principals and your school board about this system. If you are a principal, share your thoughts with a core group of your most positive administrators, teachers, and parents, who will then talk to others so the idea spreads virally. If you are a teacher, talk to your colleagues about it until you find a group of like-minded teachers who want to see the school give this a try. If you are a parent or community member, start talking to others about it. I believe this idea is so powerful that, as people talk about it, it will build momentum and generate more fans until people unite behind the idea and believe that they can change the culture of their own school, one student at a time.

The Reality-Based Road Map

Our road map can turn around a failing or struggling school. I believe in this success because of the following realities that our plan encompasses. Our plan:

- Recognizes the political realities of turning around a school, including realities such as the strength of teacher unions and the scarcity of resources, such as time and money, that are inherent in the struggle

- Takes into account the psychological realities of what teachers and students need in order to be motivated to work hard at teaching and learning, especially when they feel like they have failed at it so consistently in the past

- Acknowledges the practical realities that schooling is a system and that systematic mechanisms are needed to make any changes permanent

- Recognizes the importance of interpersonal communication and teamwork among teachers, teachers and students, teachers and parents, and students and parents

- Recognizes that nothing is more important than the moment-by-moment interaction in the classroom among students and teachers and places a premium on growing teachers through adequate time for professional development that is focused on their most pressing needs

- Takes into account the reality of the need to provide strong leadership to lead change and defines the core beliefs that leaders must hold

Perhaps the most important reality of all the realities that our road map takes into account is this: all students can meet high learning standards if we build the right support systems and expect them to perform. We know this because we did it. We believe you can do it, too.

Guiding Questions

The following questions provide a comprehensive approach to designing your own school turnaround, covering the big-picture ideas that turned our school around. If you cannot answer yes with confidence to a question, then you have identified an element of change. Referring back to the appropriate chapters will provide the details of how to proceed in any area in which you determine growth is needed. If your planning for improvement is inclusive of all these questions and moves you toward confidently answering yes to all of them, you can rest assured that you are following the same road map we did, which means that you will arrive at our destination, too.

- Do you have a leader or group of leaders who can hold firm to core beliefs about learning and hold everyone responsible for doing whatever is necessary to meet high expectations for all students, while at the same time using effective strategies to move all people up on the teamwork continuum? (See chapter 2.)

- Do you have a communication and support system in which every parent, student, and teacher is engaged in working as part of a team to make sure students are doing the hard work of learning so that you are not just doing education *to* the student, but *with* the student? (See chapters 3 and 4.)

- Do you have appropriate interventions for the foundational skills of reading and writing that move students toward choosing to read for their own pleasure and power? (See chapters 5 and 6.)

- Do your students see the relevance of your curriculum to their needs, and do you use schoolwide learning tools for reading, writing, thinking, and problem solving in order to scaffold instruction across the curriculum? (See chapters 2 and 6.)

- Do you have systematic mechanisms for extending learning time for students who need it and for making sure they are attending class and working hard? (See chapter 6.)

- Does your professional development system honor the dailiness of teaching and the skills-acquisition continuum, and does it provide just-in-time learning for your staff? (See chapters 2, 4, and 6.)

- Do you have consistent strategies of sufficient scope being used, first by your leadership team and then by all staff, to change students' (and staff's) negative beliefs into motivating, positive beliefs about the power of education and their ability to claim it for their own? (See chapter 7.)

These questions get to the real core of what we did to turn around Granger. Starting with firm core beliefs, we built a system to support students, parents, and teachers. We made students responsible for doing the work to prepare themselves for life, and we provided customized interventions that fit our students' needs to help teach them the skills they lacked.

Why We Need to Change

Here is a common complaint that you might have heard from teachers or maybe, at times, from parents (maybe you even hear it quietly in your own heart if you listen carefully enough): We never used to do things this way. We didn't have to go through all this trouble in the old days. Teachers taught; kids learned; and if they didn't, well, it wasn't the school's fault.

Yes, that is true. But things change in response to demands over time. Our public schools were not originally designed to graduate 100 percent of students with high academic skills. Elementary school was not even compulsory by law in all states of our union until 1918. Before that, attending school was a privilege, not a right (Wise, 2008).

Any education beyond elementary school was a luxury, and the curriculum of high schools was designed for the elite who would go to college. Those extra, frivolous years beyond elementary education were not needed to get a well-paying job because most jobs at the turn of the twentieth century didn't require a high school diploma (Wise, 2008). Consequently, in 1910, fewer than 20 percent of Americans aged fifteen to eighteen were enrolled in high school, and out of that number, only half of them, roughly 10 percent of all American teens, graduated (Goldin & Katz, 2008). If parents had enough money, and if their kids didn't have learning disabilities or other educational disadvantages, their children could go to high school and learn basic literacy and numeracy skills along with the civics, history, and science lessons that were adequate for simpler times.

But the times changed. From 1910 to 1940, the high school movement rapidly increased enrollment in and graduation from high schools as more high schools were built and the curriculum changed from a strictly college-bound orientation to a broader curriculum designed to meet local employment and community needs. Most new schools required no entrance exams, which was a change from earlier college-prep high schools that screened applicants through entrance testing. The academic standards were also looser than the traditional prep schools. And the new high schools had another important benefit: they were free. Aided by tougher child labor laws and the Great Depression, which both took away job opportunities for teens, these open-enrollment, education-for-all high schools exploded in popularity (Goldin & Katz, 2008). By 1940, 73 percent of American teens were enrolled in high school. By 1962, enrollment was 90 percent, and roughly 70 percent of American teens were graduating from high school (Miao & Haney, 2004).

Then came the realization that Mrs. Cordoba, the mom who did her best in chapter 3, had to face. Twelve years of attendance, scraping by with a minimal grade point average and doing just enough to earn a high school diploma, was no longer good enough for the times. Current U.S. Department of Labor projections exemplify this awareness: nearly two-thirds of new jobs in the period from 2004 to 2014 will be filled by workers with at least some postsecondary education, and 90 percent of the high-paying new jobs will require a bachelor's degree (U.S. Department of Labor, 2006). Thus, in the first decade of the new millennium, the U.S. federal government and most states changed the measure of educational success from twelve years of attendance to actual academic achievement.

From the beauty of America's egalitarian idealism—equal opportunity for all our citizens through the power of education—came the idea to open our doors throughout the twentieth century to all kinds of students who had never been educated before. From the strength of that egalitarian realism—the American dream can be achieved only by those with the skills and knowledge to actualize it—we applied the same rigor that was once reserved for the elite to all students.

This clash between beauty and strength, idealism and realism, is what we feel today. As citizens, we are growing in equality. As educators, we have always grown to keep up with the challenges of new times. We are confident that we can all grow to meet the new demands.

The Best Road Map for Ending Poverty?

We mentioned David Berliner and Richard Rothstein as researchers who say that schools cannot educate today's students to high standards on their own (see chapter 2). They say that we need dramatic social change to eliminate poverty in order to accomplish educational change. We think they have it exactly backward. We need dramatic educational change that will eliminate poverty in order to accomplish social change. This statement is not meant to be political; it is neither liberal nor conservative. But we believe it is in keeping with the deepest ideals of traditional progressive education: the power to change society is contained within the walls of the classroom.

We know that poverty is not an excuse for educational failure. Our results prove that. We know it is possible for students to escape poverty in one generation through the power of education. My brothers and sisters and I are proof of that. I looked at all of our students at Granger and saw that some may not yet have had all the skills or the personal courage to take the risks to move completely out of poverty. The cycle for them had been deep and debilitating. But I know that if we as an educational community take up the same road map that we first blazed the trails for in Granger, and if we keep improving our schools, the children of our Granger students—the second generation—will be the ones to escape the cycle. I can think of no social program with as much potential as this one. We literally have the opportunity to change society by changing one life at a time.

Call to Action

I like to say, "There's no such thing as perfect people, only perfect intentions." We did not perfect the model for turnaround schools, but we got so far, against all odds, that we built a foundation for others to take it further. Like the Sputnik program, which inspired a race in space that progressed from unmanned flights to manned, then to orbiting Earth and taking space walks, and culminated with the manned moon landing, we, too, have been part of a race. We place ourselves squarely on the time line as being one of the first to get our poverty-stricken high school into orbit and keep it up there. Now it is your turn to build on our success and go even further. Go to the moon. Go to Venus and Mars and Jupiter. Go, as Buzz Lightyear would say, "to infinity and beyond."

Hasta la Victoria Siempre! (Always toward victory!)

APPENDIX

This appendix includes samples of letters we sent out to parents and students. Please feel free to reproduce and adapt them to fit your needs.

Dear Parents/Guardians:

We are implementing a new program for high school students that will help them plan for their futures and achieve greater academic success. As parents/guardians, you are a vital part of this program. Our goal is to build a partnership with you and your student's advisor that will be ongoing throughout your student's high school career. Therefore, instead of the traditional parent/teacher conferences that are usually held at this time of year, we would like to have you meet with your student's advisor so that the advisor can explain this new program to you and get your input.

We will be holding the advisor/parent conferences on _____ .

Students will be dismissed at _____ on _____ .

The following time has been reserved for you:

Student: _____ Advisor: _____

Date: _____ Time: _____

Here are some ways you can help:

1. If you must cancel or change your conference, please call the office immediately at _____ .

2. Keep your appointment unless circumstances absolutely prevent it.

3. Limit your discussion with the advisor to thirty minutes. If you need more time, you may make another appointment.

4. This meeting will be most effective if both parents AND the student attend.

5. Please be on time.

PLEASE KEEP THIS TOP PORTION AS A REMINDER OF YOUR CONFERENCE TIME.

— — — — — — — — — — — — — — — — — —

TEAR OFF AND RETURN THIS PORTION TO THE SCHOOL.

☐ We have received _____'s advisor/parent conference appointment and plan to be there on the date and time shown above.

☐ We cannot attend at the designated time. Please contact me to schedule an alternative time. You may contact me at the following phone number: _____ .

To the parents/guardians of: _____

The staff at _____ is sending you this letter to inform you of a serious concern regarding your child's education.

Your child is currently failing two or more classes at _____. The current lack of academic progress will endanger your child's chances of earning a high school diploma.

Our staff is committed to providing your child with the support and encouragement needed to gain academic success. Teachers are available before school and after school for additional academic support.

We strongly encourage your child to participate in our _____ program(s) to help ensure academic success.

If your child chooses not to participate in our program(s) and continues to fail two or more classes, then other alternative educational programs may be more suitable for his or her needs. Alternative educational programs include _____.

Your child will have until the end of the first semester to decide which educational track he or she will choose. Other factors that will be weighted in the educational decision will be current credit status, behavior, and attendance.

Thank you for understanding that we are trying to provide your child with a positive learning environment, where he or she will have the opportunity to achieve academic success.

I understand that as parents it is our responsibility to encourage our child to attend the _____ program to help raise his or her grades.

Parent/Guardian Signature: _____ Date: _____

Student Signature: _____ Date: _____

Advisor Signature: _____ Date: _____

Academic Success Referral

The staff at _____ wants ALL students to succeed and believes that academic success needs to be our only option. Therefore, any grade lower than a C will cause students to be referred to, and encouraged to attend, our before- and/or after-school Academic Success Program.

_____ has been referred to the before- and/or after-school Academic Success Program in _____.

The following teachers/programs are available before and after school to assist students with their academic success:

- **Before school Monday through Friday**

  _____

  _____

  _____

  _____

- **After school Monday through Friday**

  _____

  _____

  _____

  _____

- **All other staff available**

  _____

  _____

  _____

  _____

Student Signature: _____ Date: _____

Teacher Signature: _____ Date: _____

Advisor Signature: _____ Date: _____

Caregiver Signature: _____ Date: _____

INSTRUCTIONS FOR IMPROVEMENT: (Teachers, please attach progress report or list assignments to be completed.)

Grade Improved! Teacher Signature: _____

REFERENCES

Allington, R. L. (2002). *Big brother and the national reading curriculum: How ideology trumped evidence.* Portsmouth, NH: Heinemann.

Berliner, D. (2009). *Poverty and potential: Out-of-school factors and school success.* Boulder and Tempe, AZ: Education and the Public Interest Center & Educational Policy Research Unit. Accessed at http://epicpolicy.org/publication/poverty -and-potential on March 16, 2009.

Billmeyer, R., & Barton, M. L. (1998). *Teaching reading in the content areas: If not me, then who?* Aurora, CO: Mid-continent Research for Education and Learning.

Carson, B. (2003, December 7). Your mind can map your destiny. *Parade,* 28–30. Accessed at www.parade.com/articles/editions/2003/edition_12-07-2003 /featured_3 on May 3, 2010.

Courtney, R. (2004, August 5). Index says Granger is safest city in the county. *Yakima Herald Republic,* Voices of the Valley, pp. 1–2.

CSSR. (n.d.). The Center for Secondary School Redesign: Advisory. Accessed at www .cssr.us/advisoryN.htm on April 5, 2011.

Cummins, J. (1979, October). *Cognitive/academic language proficiency, linguistic interdependence, the optimum age question and some other matters* (Working Papers on Bilingualism No. 19). Toronto, Canada: Ontario Institute for Studies in Education.

Dillon, S. (2010, August 9). Inexperienced companies chase U.S. school funds. *New York Times.* Accessed at www.nytimes.com/2010/08/10/education/10schools.html ?_r=1&ref=education on March 13, 2011.

Duvall, R., Ormond, J., Passer, I., & HBO Pictures. (1993). *Stalin* [Motion picture]. Culver City, CA: MGM/UA Home Video.

Editorial Projects in Education. (2007). Diplomas Count 2007: Ready for what? Preparing students for college, careers, and life after high school. *Education Week, 26*(40).

Everett Area High School. (1999, January 22). The high cost of dropping out of school. *Chieftain, 76*(5), 4.

Feldman, R. S., & Prohaska, T. (1979). The student as Pygmalion: Effect of student expectation on the teacher. *Journal of Educational Psychology, 71*(4), 485–493.

Fishburne, L., Ganis, S., Hult, N., Llewelyn, D., Romersa, M. (Producers), & Atchison, D. (Director). (2006). *Akeelah and the bee* [Motion picture]. United States: Lions Gate Films.

Gale, D., Robbins, B., Tollin, M. (Producers), & Carter, T. (Director). (2005). *Coach Carter* [Motion picture]. United States: Paramount Pictures.

Gladwell, M. (2008). *Outliers: The story of success.* Boston: Little, Brown and Company.

Goldin, C., & Katz, L. F. (2008). *The race between education and technology.* Cambridge, MA: Belknap Press of Harvard University Press.

Gordon Training International. (n.d.). *Learning a new skill is easier said than done.* Accessed at www.gordontraining.com/free-workplace-articles/learning-a-new -skill-is-easier-said-than-done/ on April 5, 2011.

Grazer, B. (Producer), & Howard, R. (Director). (1995). *Apollo 13* [Motion picture]. United States: Universal Pictures.

Hamilton, J. (2008, October 2). *Think you're multitasking? Think again.* National Public Radio. Accessed at www.npr.org/templates/story/story.php?storyId=95256794 on April 5, 2011.

House, E. R., Glass, G. V., McLean, L., & Walker, D. (1978). No simple answers: Critique of the "follow through" evaluation. *Harvard Educational Review, 48*(2), 128–160.

Hrabowski, F. A., III. (2004, Spring). Leadership for a new age: Higher education's role in producing minority leaders. *Liberal Education, 90*(2), 26. Accessed at www .aacu.org/liberaleducation/le-sp04/le-sp04feature2.cfm on August 31, 2010.

Lareau, A. (2003). *Unequal childhoods: Class, race, and family life.* Berkeley: University of California Press.

Lawrence-Lightfoot, S. (2003). *The essential conversation: What parents and teachers can learn from each other.* New York: Random House.

Maslow, A. H. (1954). *Motivation and personality.* New York: HarperCollins.

Matthews, G. (n.d.). *Goals research summary.* San Rafael: Dominican University of California. Accessed at www.dominican.edu/academics/ahss/psych /faculty/fulltime/gailmatthews/researchsummary2.pdf on September 5, 2010.

Matthews, J. (1989). *Escalante: The best teacher in America.* New York: Henry Holt and Company.

McCormack, M. (1984). *What they don't teach you at Harvard Business School.* New York: Bantam Books.

Miao, J., & Haney, W. (2004, October 15). High school graduation rates: Alternative methods and implications. *Education Policy Analysis Archives, 12*(55). Accessed at www.bc.edu/research/nbetpp/statements/nbr5.pdf on August 25, 2010.

Musca, T. (Producer), & Menéndez, R. (Director). (1988). *Stand and deliver* [Motion picture]. United States: Warner Brothers.

Oberg, K. (1960). Cultural shock: Adjusting to new cultural environments. *Practical Anthropology, 7,* 177–182.

Office of Superintendent of Public Instruction. (2001). *High school proficiency exam, measurements of student progress and Washington Assessment of Student Learning item analysis for released item information by passage including released selected, short answer and extended response.* Grade 10 - Reading. Spring 2001. Accessed at https://eds.ospi.k12.wa.us/WASLTestItems/Default.aspx on January 9, 2010.

Office of Superintendent of Public Instruction. (n.d.). *Navigation 101.* Accessed at www .k12.wa.us/navigation101/FAQs.aspx on April 6, 2011.

Orwell, G. (1954). *Animal farm.* New York: Harcourt, Brace.

Preskill, H., & Torres, R. T. (1999). *Evaluative inquiry for learning in organizations.* Thousand Oaks, CA: SAGE Publications.

Rapides Foundation. (2006). Eye-opening experience. *Central Louisiana High School Reform* [Newsletter]. Accessed at www.rapidesfoundation.org/site/Portals/0 /docs/HSReformNewsletter12.pdf on April 21, 2011.

Rosenthal, R., & Jacobson, L. (1968). *Pygmalion in the classroom: Teacher expectation and pupils' intellectual development.* New York: Holt, Rinehart, and Winston.

Rothstein, R. (2004). *Class and schools: Using social, economic, and educational reform to close the black-white achievement gap.* Washington, DC: Economic Policy Institute.

Scott, T. (Producer/director). (2005). *Domino* [Motion picture]. United States: New Line Cinema.

Sendak, M. (1963). *Where the wild things are.* New York: Harper & Row.

Seuss. (1954). *Horton hears a who!* New York: Random House.

Simonds, R. (Producer), & Dugan, D. (Director). (1996). *Happy Gilmore* [Motion picture]. United States: Universal Pictures.

U.S. Department of Labor. (2006). *America's dynamic workforce.* Washington, DC: Author. Accessed at www.dol.gov/asp/archive/reports/workforce2006/ADW2006 _Full_Text.pdf on September 5, 2010.

Whitehurst, G. J. (1997). Language processes in context: Language learning in children reared in poverty. In L. B. Adamson & M. A. Romski (Eds.), *Research on communication and language disorders: Contribution to theories of language development* (pp. 233–266). Baltimore, MD: Brookes.

Wise, B. (2008). High schools at the tipping point. *Educational Leadership, 65,* 8–13. Accessed at www.ascd.org/publications/educational-leadership/summer08 /v0165/num10/High-Schools-at-the-Tipping-Point.aspx on August 25, 2010.

York, E. B. (2008, February 18). Subway can't stop jonesing for Jared. *Advertising Age*. Accessed at http://adage.com/article/news/subway-stop-jonesing-jared/125142/ on April 7, 2011.

INDEX

Vocabulary Games for the Classroom
By Lindsay Carleton and Robert J. Marzano
Make direct vocabulary instruction fun and successful with this simple, straightforward, and easy-to-use book. Hundreds of vocabulary terms handpicked by Dr. Marzano cover four content areas and all grade levels.
BKL007

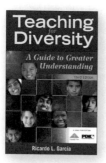

Teaching for Diversity
A Guide to Greater Understanding
By Ricardo L. García
Explore the demographic shifts in American life and schools throughout the late 20th and early 21st centuries, and examine the impact of these shifts on education. This book provides a powerful theoretical framework for thinking about and fostering acceptance of diversity and difference.
BKF400

Power Tools for Adolescent Literacy
Strategies for Learning
By Jan Rozzelle and Carol Scearce
Teachers need the right resources for engaging students in reading. This book is a veritable encyclopedia of literacy strategies secondary teachers can apply to all content areas immediately. It integrates key strategies, research from top literacy experts, and proven intervention practices.
BKF261

Pyramid Response to Intervention
RTI, Professional Learning Communities, and How to Respond When Kids Don't Learn
By Austin Buffum, Mike Mattos, and Chris Weber
Accessible language and compelling stories illustrate how RTI is most effective when built on the Professional Learning Communities at Work™ process. Written by award-winning educators, this book details three tiers of interventions—from basic to intensive—and includes implementation ideas.
BKF251

Visit solution-tree.com or call 800.733.6786 to order.

Solution Tree | Press